AI Digest

**Everything you wanted to
know about AI
but don't have time to read**

VOLUME 1

Dr Darryl J Carlton

Technics Publications
SEDONA, ARIZONA

115 Linda Vista
Sedona, AZ 86336 USA
https://www.TechnicsPub.com

Edited by Sadie Hoberman

Cover design by Lorena Molinari

First Printing 2024

Copyright © 2024 by Dr Darryl J Carlton

ISBN, print ed.   9781634625241
ISBN, Kindle ed.   9781634625258
ISBN, PDF ed.   9781634625265

Contents

From the Author

Many clever and dedicated people worldwide contribute to the rapid development of Artificial Intelligence (AI). The volume of information bombarding us is impossible to keep up with.

From my youth, I recall my father getting his regular copy of Readers Digest—an anthology of condensed books. This allowed the time-poor reader to keep up with their reading even if they did not have time for the complete published works.

In the spirit of readers' digest, I am producing a condensed version of critical research and thinking on topics related to artificial intelligence. This digest of condensed material will supplement the originals, not replace them.

Each essay is both a summary of the original plus some analysis to provide guidance as to what the original article was intending to say to us, the reader.

I hope that by quickly "skimming" the key concepts in the condensed and summarized versions, you, the reader, can find the research articles and opinion pieces of the greatest importance to you and your work and focus on those.

I do not intend for you to read these Volumes (I am currently planning three) cover-to-cover. Instead, flick through the table of contents and find the articles that interest you. Use the AI Digest as a reference book for issues you face when engaging in an Informed Discussion.

I wish you all the best in your knowledge journey.

Darryl Carlton
darryl.carlton@me.com
https://www.darrylcarlton.com

One

The EU made a deal on AI rules: But can regulators move at the speed of tech?

Atlantic Council, 11th December 2023

The European Union has reached a political agreement on the world's first comprehensive artificial intelligence regulations, known as the AI Act. This landmark legislation aims to regulate AI technologies based on their level of risk, with transparency requirements for "limited risk" AI systems and outright bans on "unacceptable risk" AI tools. While the full details are still emerging, the AI Act represents a significant shift in the global AI regulatory landscape, with far-reaching implications for technology firms operating in or selling to the EU market.

This report analyzes the key provisions of the AI Act, examines its potential impact on the AI industry, and provides strategic guidance for technology leaders navigating this new regulatory environment.

Key Findings

- The AI Act establishes a risk-based approach to AI regulation, with varying requirements based on an AI system's potential for harm.

- Implementation of the Act is not expected until 2025, raising concerns about its ability to keep pace with rapid advancements in AI technology.

- The Act aims to protect citizens from AI abuses while still allowing for innovation, mirroring aspirations expressed in recent US AI initiatives.

- Significant carve-outs and exemptions, particularly for law enforcement and national security, may create potential for abuse.

- The Act's success will depend heavily on vigorous enforcement and adequate funding for the new EU AI Office.

- Environmental impact reporting for AI systems may be included, potentially setting a global precedence.

Analysis

Strategic Planning Assumptions

- By 2026, 80% of large technology firms will have dedicated AI Act compliance teams integrated into their product development processes.

- Through 2027, at least five major European Court of Justice rulings will clarify key AI Act provisions due to implementation disputes.

- By 2028, at least three non-EU jurisdictions will implement regulations closely modeled on the EU AI Act.

Market Impact

The AI Act introduces significant market uncertainties and opportunities:

- **Competitive Landscape:** The Act may inadvertently benefit larger, more established AI providers who have the resources to navigate complex compliance requirements. Smaller EU-based AI startups may face challenges in competing with global tech giants.

- **Innovation Dynamics:** While aiming to foster responsible AI development, stringent regulations may slow the pace of innovation in some areas. Conversely, regulatory clarity could attract AI investment to the EU market.

- **Global Influence:** As the first comprehensive AI regulation, the AI Act is likely to influence similar legislation worldwide, potentially leading to a "Brussels Effect" in AI governance.

Risk-Based Approach

The AI Act categorizes AI systems based on their potential risk:

- **Unacceptable Risk:** Systems posing threats to safety, livelihoods, or rights will be banned. Examples include social scoring by governments and emotion recognition in workplaces or educational institutions.

- **High Risk:** Systems used in critical infrastructure, education, employment, essential private and public services, law enforcement, migration, and justice administration will face strict obligations. Requirements include risk assessments, high-quality datasets, logging of activity, detailed documentation, clear user information, human oversight, and robust security.

- **Limited Risk:** Systems like chatbots will be subject to transparency requirements, ensuring users know they are interacting with an AI.

- **Minimal or No Risk:** The vast majority of AI systems will fall into this category and be freely used with no restrictions.

Key Provisions and Implications

- **Law Enforcement Use:** The Act allows limited use of remote biometric identification systems by law enforcement in public spaces, with safeguards. This compromise attempts to balance public safety concerns with civil liberties protections.

- **Generative AI:** Large language models and other foundation models will face transparency and documentation requirements. Providers must disclose training data sources and demonstrate efforts to respect copyright law.

- **Environmental Impact:** The Act may include provisions for reporting the ecological impact of AI systems, potentially setting a global precedent for considering AI's environmental footprint.

Implementation Challenges

Several factors may complicate the AI Act's implementation:

- **Rapid Technological Advancement:** With the Act not taking effect until 2025, there are concerns about its ability to keep pace with AI innovation.

- **Enforcement Resources:** The success of the Act will depend on vigorous enforcement, requiring adequate funding and staffing for the new EU AI Office.

- **Global Regulatory Landscape:** The interaction between the AI Act and other digital regulations, such as the Digital Services Act and Digital Markets Act, remains to be fully understood.

Strategic Implications

For AI providers:

- Compliance will become a key differentiator, potentially favoring larger, well-resourced companies.

- Opportunities may arise for compliance-as-a-service offerings and AI governance tools.

- EU-based AI companies may gain a "regulatory home advantage" but could face challenges scaling globally.

For AI users:

- Organizations will need to carefully assess the risk levels of AI systems they deploy.

- Increased transparency may boost trust in AI systems but could also reveal limitations.

- Compliance costs may be passed down to end-users, potentially impacting AI adoption rates.

For policymakers:

- The AI Act will likely serve as a template for other jurisdictions considering AI regulation.

- Balancing innovation with protection will be an ongoing challenge as AI capabilities evolve.

- International regulatory cooperation will be crucial to avoid fragmentation of the global AI market.

Recommendations

Conduct an AI Act readiness assessment:

- Map existing AI systems and development pipelines against the Act's risk categories.

- Identify compliance gaps and prioritize remediation efforts.

- Engage legal experts to interpret ambiguous provisions.

Develop a compliance roadmap:

- Establish cross-functional teams to oversee AI Act compliance efforts.

- Create clear processes for assessing AI Act implications of new products and features.

- Implement robust documentation and audit trails to demonstrate good-faith compliance.

Enhance transparency and explainability:

- Invest in tools and methodologies to improve AI model interpretability.

- Develop user-friendly interfaces for presenting AI system information to end-users.

- Create comprehensive data governance frameworks to support transparency requirements.

Engage with regulators and industry groups:

- Proactively communicate compliance plans and challenges to EU regulators.

- Participate in industry working groups to develop common standards and best practices.

- Monitor and contribute to public consultations on AI Act implementation guidelines.

Align global AI strategy:

- Assess the feasibility of extending AI Act-compliant features to non-EU markets.

- Monitor regulatory developments in other jurisdictions for potential AI Act-inspired legislation.

- Develop flexible global product strategy adaptable to varied regulatory requirements.

Conclusion

The EU AI Act represents a watershed moment in the regulation of artificial intelligence. While implementation challenges remain, forward-thinking firms can turn AI Act compliance into a strategic advantage. By embracing the spirit of the regulation and proactively adapting their AI governance practices, companies can position themselves for success in the evolving global AI landscape.

As one expert put it, "The EU is boldly going where no regulator has gone before–let's hope they've packed their towel and know where their AI is." Indeed, as we venture into this brave new world of AI regulation, a healthy dose of humor (and a good legal team) may be just what the algorithm ordered.

Technology leaders who approach the AI Act strategically–viewing it not just as a compliance exercise but as a catalyst for responsible innovation–will be best positioned to thrive in this new regulatory environment. As the digital economy continues to evolve, the ability to navigate complex regulatory frameworks while delivering value to users will become an increasingly critical competitive differentiator.

Two

The competitive relationship between cloud computing and generative AI

Bruegel - European Think Tank in Economics, 11ᵗʰ December 2023

The rapid evolution of cloud computing and generative artificial intelligence (GenAI) is reshaping the technological landscape, creating a symbiotic relationship that promises significant innovation but also raises complex competitive concerns. This report analyzes the intricate dynamics between cloud providers and GenAI developers, highlighting both the opportunities for growth and the potential risks to fair competition. As these technologies become increasingly central to digital transformation strategies, organizations must navigate a complex regulatory environment while leveraging the benefits of this powerful technological convergence.

Key Findings

- Cloud providers and GenAI developers have formed a mutually beneficial ecosystem, with cloud infrastructure enabling GenAI innovation and GenAI driving cloud service adoption.

- Partnerships between cloud and GenAI providers, particularly involving hyperscalers, are intensifying market concentration and raising competitive concerns.

- Potential anticompetitive practices include discriminatory IT supply, interoperability barriers, data exploitation, self-preferencing, and tying/bundling strategies.

- Current regulatory frameworks, including EU's Digital Markets Act (DMA) and Data Act, address some but not all competitive risks in this rapidly evolving sector.

- Proactive monitoring and targeted regulatory interventions are necessary to maintain a balanced, innovative market environment.

Analysis

Market Implications

The cloud-GenAI relationship is reshaping market dynamics across multiple sectors:

- **Cloud Infrastructure:** Demand for specialized AI-optimized infrastructure is skyrocketing, benefiting providers with large-scale capabilities but potentially marginalizing smaller players.

- **Software Development:** GenAI is revolutionizing software creation, with cloud-based AI development platforms becoming essential tools for developers.

- **Enterprise Productivity:** Integration of GenAI into cloud-based productivity suites is redefining workplace efficiency and collaboration.

- **Data Analytics:** Cloud-powered GenAI is transforming data analysis capabilities, making advanced insights more accessible to a broader range of organizations.

Strategic Planning Assumptions

- By 2025, 60% of enterprise AI workloads will run on cloud infrastructure specifically optimized for AI computation.

- Through 2026, at least three major antitrust cases related to cloud-GenAI partnerships will be initiated by global regulatory bodies.

- By 2027, 40% of new enterprise software applications will be developed using GenAI tools integrated into cloud development platforms.

The Symbiotic Cloud-GenAI Relationship

Cloud computing and GenAI have formed a symbiotic relationship that is driving rapid innovation and market growth. Cloud providers offer the massive computing power and scalable infrastructure essential for training and deploying complex AI models. In return, GenAI applications are becoming significant drivers of cloud service adoption and revenue growth.

This relationship manifests across all layers of the cloud stack:

- **Infrastructure as a Service (IaaS):** GenAI providers rely on cloud infrastructure for flexible, scalable computing resources. Major cloud players are investing heavily in AI-optimized hardware and exclusive partnerships with leading AI firms.

- **Platform as a Service (PaaS):** Cloud providers are integrating GenAI capabilities into their development platforms, enabling the creation of AI-powered applications and services.

- **Software as a Service (SaaS):** GenAI is being woven into cloud-based productivity suites and enterprise applications, enhancing functionality and user experience.

Competitive Landscape and Risks

While this synergy is driving innovation, it also raises significant competitive concerns:

- **Market Concentration:** Partnerships between major cloud providers (hyperscalers) and leading GenAI developers are intensifying market concentration. This trend could make it increasingly difficult for smaller players to compete effectively.

- **Interoperability Barriers:** Proprietary AI-cloud integrations may create significant switching costs for customers, potentially leading to vendor lock-in.

- **Data Exploitation:** Cloud providers' access to vast amounts of customer data could be leveraged unfairly to develop competing AI services.

- **Self-Preferencing:** Cloud platforms may prioritize their own AI services over third-party offerings, distorting fair competition.

- **Tying and Bundling:** Dominant players could leverage their market power in one sector (e.g., productivity software) to gain advantages in cloud or AI markets.

Regulatory Landscape

Current regulatory frameworks are struggling to keep pace with the rapid evolution of the cloud-GenAI ecosystem. Key regulatory developments include:

- **EU Digital Markets Act (DMA):** While addressing some digital market competition issues, the DMA does not currently designate any cloud computing services as "gatekeepers."

- **EU Data Act:** Aims to improve data portability and interoperability in cloud services, but lacks clear definitions for GenAI applications.

- **Merger Control:** Traditional definitions of "control" in merger regulations may not adequately capture the competitive influence of strategic partnerships in this space.

- **Antitrust Laws:** While capable of addressing some anticompetitive practices, these laws may struggle with the complex, rapidly evolving nature of cloud-GenAI relationships.

To address these regulatory gaps, policymakers should consider:

- Expanding the definition of "concentration" in merger control to include material competitive influence, even without formal control.

- Clarifying and strengthening interoperability requirements in the Data Act, with a focus on GenAI applications.

- Developing new frameworks for assessing competitive impacts in AI-driven markets.

Recommendations

Conduct a cloud-AI strategy audit:

- Assess current and planned use of cloud and GenAI technologies.

- Identify potential lock-in risks and develop multi-cloud contingency plans.

- Evaluate partnerships between your cloud providers and GenAI developers for potential competitive impacts.

Prioritize interoperability and data portability:

- Implement strict data governance policies to maintain control over proprietary information.

- Invest in solutions that support seamless data and workload migration between cloud providers.

- Advocate for industry-wide interoperability standards for GenAI models and applications.

Develop in-house AI expertise:

- Cultivate internal AI capabilities to reduce overreliance on single-vendor solutions.

- Create cross-functional teams to oversee AI governance and ethical considerations.

- Invest in ongoing AI literacy programs for all levels of the organization.

Monitor regulatory developments:

- Stay informed about evolving antitrust and AI governance legislation.

- Participate in industry consortia to influence policy development.

- Prepare compliance strategies for upcoming regulations like the EU's AI Act.

Leverage multi-cloud strategies:

- Diversify cloud service providers to mitigate vendor lock-in risks.

- Explore specialized AI cloud services to complement general-purpose offerings.

- Develop a clear exit strategy for each cloud service to maintain flexibility.

Conclusion

The Cloud-GenAI nexus presents immense opportunities for innovation and economic growth. However, realizing this potential while maintaining a fair and competitive market requires a delicate balance. Organizations must strategically leverage these technologies while remaining vigilant about potential lock-in and competitive risks. Regulators, for their part, must evolve their frameworks to address the unique challenges posed by this rapidly advancing ecosystem.

As one industry pundit quipped, "In the cloud-AI gold rush, it's not just about who has the biggest shovel, but who can dig without causing an avalanche." Indeed, the winners in this new landscape will be those who can harness the power of cloud and GenAI technologies while navigating the complex competitive and regulatory terrain.

By fostering a diverse, interoperable ecosystem and implementing thoughtful guardrails, we can ensure that the cloud-GenAI revolution drives innovation that benefits businesses and society at large, rather than consolidating power in the hands of a few tech giants. The future of computing is undoubtedly in the clouds, but it's up to us to ensure it's a sky where many stars can shine.

THREE

Policymakers should use the SETI model to prepare for AI doomsday scenarios

Center for Data Innovation, Daniel Castro, 4th December 2023

The development of Artificial General Intelligence (AGI) remains a topic of intense debate and speculation within the tech industry and beyond. While some experts warn of existential risks, others remain skeptical about the near-term feasibility of AGI. This report examines the current landscape, potential risks, and proposed approaches to managing AGI development, with a focus on balancing innovation with responsible governance.

Key Findings

- **AGI Development Timeline:** There is no consensus on when or if AGI will be achieved. Predictions range from imminent breakthroughs to decades or more of continued research.

- **Risk Assessment:** While some experts warn of catastrophic risks, others view these concerns as premature or exaggerated. The hypothetical nature of AGI risks complicates traditional risk assessment methodologies.

- **Regulatory Approaches:** Proposed measures range from research moratoriums to international oversight bodies. However, premature or overly restrictive regulations could stifle beneficial AI innovations.

- **Geopolitical Considerations:** AI development has become a key area of technological competition between nations, particularly the United States and China. This complicates efforts for international cooperation on AGI safety.

- **Industry Initiatives:** Leading AI companies and research institutions increasingly invest in AI safety research and ethical AI development practices.

Analysis

The debate surrounding AGI development and its potential risks has intensified in recent years, fueled by rapid advancements in AI capabilities and high-profile warnings from some industry leaders. However, it's crucial to approach this topic with a balanced perspective, recognizing both the potential benefits and risks of advanced AI systems.

Current State of AGI Research

AGI, sometimes referred to as "human-level AI" or "strong AI," remains a theoretical concept. While narrow AI systems have achieved remarkable capabilities in specific domains, we have yet to create AI systems that possess the general problem-solving abilities and adaptability of human intelligence.

Example: While an AI system like AlphaGo can outperform human champions at the game of Go, it cannot transfer that intelligence to other tasks like driving a car or writing a novel–capabilities that would be expected of an AGI system.

Risk Assessment Challenges

The hypothetical nature of AGI makes traditional risk assessment methodologies challenging to apply. Some experts argue that the potential for an intelligence explosion, where an AGI system rapidly improves itself beyond human control, poses an existential risk to humanity. Others view these concerns as premature or based on flawed assumptions about AI development trajectories.

Example: The difficulty in assessing AGI risks is similar to evaluating the risks of contact with extraterrestrial intelligence. Both scenarios involve high-impact but highly uncertain outcomes, making allocating resources and developing concrete policy responses challenging.

Regulatory Approaches

Proposed regulatory measures for AGI range from research moratoriums to international oversight bodies. However, implementing effective regulations for a technology that doesn't yet exist presents significant challenges.

Example: The proposal for an "International Atomic Energy Agency (IAEA) for AI" demonstrates the tendency to draw parallels with other potentially dangerous technologies. However, unlike nuclear technology, AI development is more distributed and less centralized, making such a regulatory model potentially less effective.

The SAGI Institute Proposal

The concept of a Search for Artificial General Intelligence (SAGI) Institute offers a promising middle ground between inaction and overregulation. By focusing on developing consensus around AGI detection and response protocols, this approach allows for continued innovation while establishing a framework for monitoring potential breakthroughs.

Example: Just as SETI researchers have developed protocols for detecting and responding to potential signs of extraterrestrial intelligence, a SAGI Institute could establish similar guidelines for identifying and verifying AGI capabilities.

Balancing Innovation and Responsibility

As AI capabilities continue to advance, it's crucial to strike a balance between fostering innovation and addressing potential risks. This requires ongoing collaboration between researchers, industry leaders, policymakers, and ethicists.

Example: Many leading AI companies have established internal ethics boards and are investing in AI safety research. Encouraging and expanding these voluntary initiatives can complement more formal regulatory approaches.

Recommendations

- **Establish a Search for Artificial General Intelligence (SAGI) Institute:** Modeled after the Search for Extra-Terrestrial Intelligence (SETI) Institute, this organization would focus on developing consensus around signs of AGI, testing methodologies, and response protocols.

- **Promote Voluntary Industry Cooperation:** Encourage AI developers to collaborate with the SAGI Institute, share research findings, and submit to AGI detection protocols.

- **Foster International Collaboration:** Despite geopolitical tensions, pursue opportunities for scientific cooperation on AGI research and safety measures.

- **Balance Regulation and Innovation:** Avoid premature or overly broad regulations that could hinder beneficial AI development. Focus on specific use cases and applications rather than speculative future scenarios.

- **Invest in AI Safety Research:** Continue to support and expand research into AI alignment, robustness, and ethical considerations across existing and emerging AI models.

Conclusion

The development of Artificial General Intelligence remains a topic of intense speculation and debate. While the potential risks associated with AGI should not be dismissed, it's equally important to avoid premature or overly restrictive measures that could hinder beneficial AI innovations. The proposed SAGI Institute offers a pragmatic approach to monitoring AGI development while allowing continued research and innovation. As the field evolves, ongoing collaboration between stakeholders will be essential to responsibly navigate the complex landscape of advanced AI development.

FOUR

Quantum technologies and cybersecurity in the EU: There's still a long way to go

Center for European Policy Studies, 6th December 2023

The rapid advancement of quantum technologies presents both unprecedented opportunities and significant challenges for cybersecurity. This report examines the current state of quantum computing, its potential impact on cryptography, and the strategic considerations for organizations and policymakers as they prepare for a post-quantum world.

Key Findings

- **Quantum Revolution:** We are in the midst of a quantum revolution, with breakthroughs enabling direct manipulation of quantum systems and the development of quantum-based technologies.

- **Dual-Use Nature:** Quantum technologies offer tremendous benefits across sectors but also pose significant risks to current cybersecurity paradigms.

- **Cryptographic Threat:** Cryptographically Relevant Quantum Computers (CRQCs) could break widely used encryption algorithms, potentially compromising data confidentiality and integrity across the internet.

- **Timeline Uncertainty:** While fully capable CRQCs are not expected for 5-30 years, the "hack now, decrypt later" threat necessitates proactive preparation.

- **Quantum-Resistant Solutions:** Quantum-resistant cryptography is being developed but requires careful implementation and a potentially complex transition period.

- **EU Position:** Europe is a leader in quantum technology funding but lags in policies for quantum-resistant cryptography adoption.

Analysis

The Quantum Revolution

Quantum technologies leverage the principles of quantum mechanics to perform computations and manipulations at the subatomic level. This paradigm shift offers unprecedented computational power for certain classes of problems.

Example: A quantum computer with just 20 million qubits could potentially break encryption codes in hours that would take classical supercomputers trillions of years to crack.

Cybersecurity Implications

While quantum technologies promise advancements in various fields, they pose a significant threat to current cryptographic systems. Most internet security relies on algorithms that could be vulnerable to quantum attacks.

Example: Public key encryption, widely used for secure communication and digital signatures, could be compromised by sufficiently powerful quantum computers.

The "Hack Now, Decrypt Later" Threat

Even before fully capable quantum computers are available, adversaries may collect and store encrypted data with the intention of decrypting it once quantum capabilities mature.

Example: Sensitive government or corporate communications intercepted today could be decrypted years later, potentially compromising long-term strategic interests.

Quantum-Resistant Cryptography

Researchers are developing new cryptographic algorithms designed to resist quantum attacks. However, transitioning to these new standards presents significant challenges.

Example: The US National Institute of Standards and Technology (NIST) is leading efforts to standardize post-quantum cryptographic algorithms, but widespread adoption will take time and careful planning.

EU's Quantum Position

While Europe is a leader in quantum technology funding, it lags behind in policies for quantum-resistant cryptography adoption and quantum vulnerability assessment.

Example: The EU has invested approximately €10 billion in quantum technologies since 2016, but lacks comprehensive strategies for migrating critical infrastructure to quantum-resistant systems.

Cryptographic Agility

Organizations need to develop the ability to quickly update cryptographic protocols in response to evolving threats.

Example: Implementing crypto-agile systems now can facilitate smoother transitions to quantum-resistant algorithms in the future.

Quantum AI and Future Applications

The combination of quantum computing and artificial intelligence could lead to powerful new capabilities in data analysis and prediction.

Example: Quantum machine learning algorithms could analyze complex datasets far more efficiently than classical methods, leading to breakthroughs in drug discovery or financial modeling.

Responsible Governance

As quantum technologies mature, it's crucial to develop frameworks for their ethical and responsible deployment.

Example: Ensuring equitable access to quantum technologies and preventing their use for malicious purposes will require coordinated international efforts.

Recommendations

- **Accelerate Quantum-Resistant Cryptography:** Prioritize research, development, and standardization of quantum-resistant cryptographic algorithms.

- **Implement Cryptographic Agility:** Design systems with the flexibility to rapidly adopt new cryptographic protocols as quantum threats evolve.

- **Conduct Quantum Risk Assessments:** Organizations should evaluate their cryptographic vulnerabilities and develop transition plans.

- **Foster International Collaboration:** Promote global cooperation on quantum security standards and best practices.

- **Invest in Quantum Skills:** Address the talent gap by supporting education and training programs in quantum technologies and cybersecurity.

- **Develop Responsible Governance:** Establish frameworks for the ethical development and deployment of quantum technologies.

Conclusion

The quantum revolution presents a double-edged sword for cybersecurity. While quantum technologies offer immense potential for advancing various fields, they also pose significant risks to current cryptographic systems. Organizations and policymakers must act now to prepare for the post-quantum era, investing in quantum-resistant cryptography, fostering international collaboration, and developing responsible governance frameworks.

The transition to a quantum-secure future will be complex and challenging, requiring careful planning, substantial investment, and ongoing adaptation. However, by taking proactive steps today, we can harness the benefits of quantum technologies while mitigating their potential risks to cybersecurity.

As we navigate this new frontier, continued research, collaboration, and strategic foresight will be essential to ensuring a secure and prosperous quantum future.

In tech, the death of the Brussels Effect is greatly exaggerated

Center for European Reform, Zach Meyers, 8th December 2023

Despite challenges from the US and post-Brexit Britain, the European Union's influence on global technology regulations—known as the "Brussels Effect"—remains strong. This report examines the current state of EU tech regulation, its global impact, and strategic considerations for policymakers and businesses navigating this regulatory landscape.

Key Findings

- **Enduring Influence:** The EU's regulatory power in the tech sector persists, driven by its significant share of global services imports and the interconnected nature of digital services.

- **Digital Services Focus:** The Brussels Effect may be particularly pronounced for digital services due to the difficulty of market segmentation and the EU's importance as an export destination.

- **Regulatory Quality:** Foreign governments often model their laws on EU regulations due to their perceived high quality and focus on widely accepted principles.

- **Self-Sabotage Risks:** Some EU regulatory approaches, particularly in data protection, risk undermining the Brussels Effect by forcing segmentation of services.

- **US and UK Adaptation:** Major economies like the US and UK are finding they must engage with EU regulations rather than pursue fully independent approaches.

- **Economic Impact:** The EU's regulatory influence does not necessarily hinder its economic growth, as evidenced by successes in areas like green industries.

Analysis

The Persistence of the Brussels Effect

Despite predictions of its decline, the EU's ability to shape global tech regulations remains robust. This influence stems from several factors:

- **Market Size and Importance:** The EU's share of global services imports has grown to about 30%, making it an "unavoidable trading destination" for many tech firms.

- **Example:** Major US tech companies like Meta and Apple derive 22-24% of their revenue from Europe, making it their most important foreign market.

- **Digital Services Dynamics:** Unlike goods producers, digital service providers often need help to easily divert their offerings to alternative markets, increasing their susceptibility to EU regulations.

- **Example:** Social networks and AI foundation models benefit from a global scale, making EU-only variants less desirable or technically complex to implement.

- **Regulatory Quality and Acceptance:** EU regulations are often seen as high-quality compromises addressing widely accepted issues, making them attractive models for other jurisdictions.

- **Example:** EU digital laws typically focus on fundamental rights and competition principles rather than narrow European economic interests.

Challenges to the Brussels Effect

While the EU's regulatory influence remains strong, several factors could potentially weaken it:

- **Self-Imposed Limitations:** Some EU regulations, particularly in data protection, force companies to treat European data differently, potentially undermining global regulatory convergence.

> **Example:** Strict interpretations of GDPR data transfer rules make it increasingly difficult for companies to maintain unified global data practices.

- **Innovation Friction:** Regulations that hinder popular services or innovations may lead companies to limit their EU offerings, reducing the global impact of those rules.

- **Example:** Meta's decision not to launch its Threads platform in the EU due to concerns about upcoming digital competition laws.

- **Protectionist Perceptions:** If EU regulations are seen as primarily serving European economic interests rather than addressing universal concerns, their global appeal may diminish.

Strategic Implications for Global Players

US: The US faces the challenge of influencing EU tech regulations while maintaining its own regulatory approach. Current efforts, such as voluntary AI commitments and executive orders, may need to be revised against more comprehensive EU laws.

Recommendation: Reinvigorate engagement through forums like the EU-US Trade and Technology Council to shape EU regulatory approaches.

UK: Post-Brexit, the UK aims to create a more agile regulatory environment but remains heavily dependent on EU markets, particularly for ICT services exports.

Recommendation: Pursue closer coordination with EU regulators to influence outcomes rather than focusing on minor regulatory divergences.

Recommendations

- **Prioritize Consumer-Centric Regulation:** EU policymakers should focus on regulations that deliver clear benefits to consumers to maintain global influence.

- **Maintain Market Openness:** Avoid protectionist measures that could undermine the perception of EU regulations as high-quality and universally applicable.

- **Enhance Regulatory Interoperability:** Design rules with global applicability in mind to prevent fragmentation of digital services.

- **Engage in International Dialogue:** The US and UK should focus on influencing EU regulatory approaches rather than pursuing divergent paths.

- **Streamline Intra-EU Consistency:** Address risks of inconsistent application of regulations across EU member states to maintain the single market's power.

- **Balance Innovation and Regulation:** Carefully apply rules in areas like AI and digital competition to avoid hindering valuable innovations.

Conclusion

The Brussels Effect in tech regulation shows remarkable resilience, driven by the EU's market importance and the global nature of digital services. While challenges exist, the EU's ability to shape global tech standards is likely to persist if it maintains a focus on consumer benefits, market openness, and regulatory interoperability.

For global tech firms and policymakers, the key to success lies in engaging constructively with EU regulatory processes rather than seeking to circumvent them. As digital technologies continue to evolve, the EU's regulatory approach will remain a critical factor in shaping the global tech landscape.

Six

The AI assault on women: What Iran's tech enabled morality laws indicate for women's rights movements

Council on Foreign Relations, Rachel George, 7th December 2023

Iran's use of AI-assisted repression against the "Women, Life, Freedom" movement highlights a growing threat to women's rights globally. This report examines the Iranian government's deployment of AI technologies to enforce strict morality codes, the broader implications for women's rights movements, and recommendations for addressing this emerging challenge.

Key Findings

- **AI-Enabled Repression:** Iran has leveraged AI-facilitated practices, including facial recognition, geolocation, and web traffic analysis to crack down on women's rights protesters.

- **Legislative Support:** The Iranian government introduced draft legislation explicitly committing to using AI-assisted tools to enforce morality codes.

- **Scale of Impact:** Over 20,000 arrests and 500 protester deaths have been reported, with over one million women receiving warnings about dress code violations detected by AI systems.

- **Regional Concerns:** Other Middle Eastern countries with male guardianship laws could potentially use similar technologies to restrict women's mobility and freedoms.

- **International Involvement:** Chinese exports of surveillance technology to Iran have doubled, raising concerns about the spread of repressive capabilities.

- **Broader Implications:** AI-assisted gender repression threatens not only women's rights but also wider security and democratization efforts in the region.

Analysis

The Iranian Case Study

Iran's deployment of AI technologies to enforce strict morality codes represents a significant escalation in the tools available to authoritarian regimes for suppressing women's rights movements.

Example: The use of facial recognition technology to identify women violating hijab laws demonstrates how AI can dramatically increase the scale and efficiency of repressive measures.

Regional Implications

The potential for AI-assisted repression to spread to other countries with restrictive gender laws is a major concern.

Example: Saudi Arabia's $400 million investment in "smart cities" technology from Huawei raises alarms about the potential for expanded surveillance and control of women's movements.

Global Technology Supply Chains

The role of international technology suppliers in enabling repressive regimes highlights the need for greater oversight and accountability.

Example: The doubling of Chinese exports of video recorders to Iran in 2022 demonstrates how quickly repressive capabilities can be enhanced through technology transfers.

Challenges to Women's Movements

AI-enabled repression presents a new and formidable obstacle to women's rights activists and pro-democracy movements.

Example: The ability to rapidly identify and target protesters through facial recognition and geolocation technologies makes organizing and participating in demonstrations far more dangerous.

International Response

The global community's reaction to AI-assisted repression will be crucial in shaping the future landscape of women's rights and civil liberties.

Example: US sanctions against Chinese company Tiandy in response to its role in Iranian surveillance show the potential for international pressure to influence technology exports.

Recommendations

- **Enhance Monitoring and Reporting:** Increase independent, credible reporting on the use of technology for political repression, particularly against women's movements.

- **Prioritize AI Governance:** Focus AI ethics and governance debates on mitigating the risks of gender-based repression.

- **Corporate Responsibility:** Western companies must develop safeguards to prevent their technologies from being used for repression.

- **Sanctions and Accountability:** Consider new sanctions against companies whose technologies support repressive surveillance.

- **Media Engagement:** Encourage international media to expose cases of AI-enabled repression and rights abuses.

- **Strengthen International Guidelines:** Develop explicit norms and guidelines banning the use of AI for gendered repression in domestic settings.

- **Expand Existing Frameworks:** Build upon UNESCO's Recommendation on the Ethics of AI and UN resolutions to address AI-assisted surveillance for gender repression.

Conclusion

The use of AI technologies to enforce repressive gender laws in Iran represents a critical juncture for women's rights movements globally. As these technologies become more sophisticated and widely available, there is an urgent need for concerted international action to prevent their misuse.

Key steps include:

- Developing robust monitoring and reporting mechanisms to track the use of AI for repression.

- Establishing clear international norms and guidelines prohibiting the use of AI for gender-based repression.

- Holding technology companies accountable for the end-use of their products.

- Supporting media and civil society efforts to expose and combat AI-enabled repression.

By taking proactive measures now, the international community can work to ensure that advances in AI technology support, rather than undermine, the cause of women's rights and human freedom globally.

SEVEN

Plato, love, and the philosophical problem of Europe's AI Act

European Centre for International Political Economy, Fredrik Erixon,
December 2023

The European Union's forthcoming Artificial Intelligence Act (AI Act) represents a significant attempt to regulate AI technologies. However, as this analysis highlights, the lack of a clear definition for AI and the combination of multiple regulatory approaches have led to a complex and potentially problematic framework. This report examines the challenges in defining and regulating AI, drawing parallels with philosophical discussions about abstract concepts, and explores the potential implications of the EU's current approach.

Key Findings

- **Definition Challenges:** The EU needs help to establish a consistent and agreed-upon definition of AI, leading to shifting regulatory targets.

- **Regulatory Complexity:** The AI Act combines multiple regulatory approaches, including product safety, fundamental rights, and precautionary principles, resulting in a complex framework.

- **Philosophical Underpinnings:** The article draws parallels between defining AI and abstract philosophical concepts like love, highlighting the difficulty in regulating something without a clear essence.

- **Overlapping Regulations:** The AI Act's multiple regulatory cultures may lead to confusion and conflicts in practical application.

- **Innovation Concerns:** The complexity and breadth of the regulation raise concerns about potential impacts on innovation in the AI sector.

Analysis

Strategic Implications

- **Regulatory Uncertainty:** The lack of a clear AI definition may lead to uncertainty for businesses and innovators about which technologies fall under the regulation.

- **Compliance Challenges:** The overlapping regulatory approaches could make compliance complex and costly for AI developers and users.

- **Global Competitiveness:** Overly broad or complex regulations may put EU-based AI companies at a competitive disadvantage in the global market.

- **Ethical Considerations:** While attempting to address ethical concerns, the regulation's complexity may inadvertently create new ethical challenges in AI development and deployment.

- **Adaptability Issues:** AI technology's rapidly evolving nature may outpace the static regulatory framework, potentially leading to obsolescence or hindering innovation.

The Definitional Dilemma

The EU's struggle to define AI reflects the broader challenge of regulating an emerging and rapidly evolving technology.

Example: The shifting definitions used by various EU bodies and expert groups demonstrate the difficulty in pinning down a consistent concept of AI for regulatory purposes.

Regulatory Approach Conflicts

The combination of product safety, fundamental rights, and precautionary principles in the AI Act creates a complex regulatory landscape.

Example: An AI system might comply with product safety standards but still raise concerns under the fundamental rights doctrine, creating potential conflicts in enforcement and compliance.

Philosophical Underpinnings

Drawing parallels with Plato's Symposium highlights the challenge of regulating something without a clear, agreed-upon essence.

Example: Just as the symposium participants struggled to define love, policymakers face similar challenges in defining the essence of AI for regulatory purposes.

Innovation and Competitiveness Concerns

The complexity and potential overreach of the AI Act raise concerns about its impact on innovation and the competitiveness of EU-based AI companies.

Example: Stringent regulations might discourage AI startups from establishing themselves in the EU, potentially leading to a "brain drain" in the AI sector.

Adaptability to Technological Progress

The static nature of regulatory frameworks may struggle to keep pace with the rapid advancements in AI technology.

Example: By the time the AI Act is fully implemented, new forms of AI not considered during its drafting may have emerged, potentially rendering parts of the regulation obsolete or ineffective.

Recommendations

- **Refine AI Definition:** Work towards a more precise and adaptable definition of AI that can evolve with technological advancements.

- **Streamline Regulatory Approach:** Consider consolidating the multiple regulatory approaches into a more cohesive framework to reduce complexity and potential conflicts.

- **Enhance Flexibility:** Incorporate mechanisms for regular review and updates to the regulation to ensure it remains relevant as AI technology evolves.

- **Prioritize Innovation:** Balance regulatory objectives with the need to foster innovation in the AI sector, potentially through regulatory sandboxes or tiered approaches based on risk levels.

- **International Collaboration:** Engage in global dialogues to work towards more harmonized AI regulations, reducing compliance burdens for companies operating internationally.

- **Ethical Framework:** Develop a clear ethical framework for AI development and deployment that can guide regulatory efforts and provide consistency across different applications.

Conclusion

The EU's AI Act represents an ambitious attempt to regulate a complex and rapidly evolving technology. However, the challenges in defining AI and combining multiple regulatory approaches have led to a framework that may be too complex and potentially detrimental to innovation. As the EU refines its approach to AI regulation, it must strive for greater clarity, flexibility, and balance between protecting citizens and fostering innovation. By addressing these challenges, the EU can develop a more effective and adaptable regulatory framework that ensures the responsible development and deployment of AI technologies while maintaining Europe's competitiveness in the global AI landscape.

EIGHT

USTR Abandons the Digital Rule Book: to China's potential benefit

Petersen Institute for International Economics, Gary Clyde Hufbauer and Megan Hogan, 11th December 2023

The US Trade Representative's (USTR) decision to suspend efforts to protect digital rights in future trade negotiations represents a significant departure from long-standing US policy. This report examines the potential consequences of this shift, particularly in relation to China's growing influence in digital trade, and explores the strategic implications for US technological leadership and economic competitiveness.

Key Findings

- **Policy Reversal:** USTR has abandoned core principles of digital trade protection that have been central to US trade policy for decades.

- **Economic Impact:** The decision threatens the competitiveness of both large and small US tech firms in global markets.

- **China's Advantage:** The policy shift potentially benefits China by creating space for its "cyber sovereignty" approach to digital governance.

- **Interagency Conflict:** The decision has created apparent discord within the US government, with State and Commerce Departments reportedly opposed.

- **Congressional Opposition:** There is bipartisan concern in Congress over the potential negative impacts of the policy change.

- **Core Principles at Risk:** Key digital trade protections, including data flow, source code protection, and localization prohibitions, are now in jeopardy.

Analysis

Strategic Implications

- **Global Digital Governance:** The US risks ceding leadership in setting global digital trade rules, potentially to China's benefit.

- **Innovation and Competitiveness:** Reduced protections could hamper US tech innovation and global competitiveness.

- **Cybersecurity Concerns:** Weakened digital trade rules could increase vulnerability to cyber attacks and forced technology transfers.

- **Economic Security:** The policy shift may undermine the economic security of the US tech sector, which employs millions of Americans.

- **Geopolitical Influence:** Abandoning digital trade protections could diminish US influence in key regions, particularly in the Indo-Pacific.

Policy Reversal and Its Consequences

The USTR's decision marks a stark departure from decades of US trade policy focused on protecting digital rights and intellectual property.

Example: Previous agreements like the USMCA included strong protections for data flows, source code, and prohibitions on localization requirements. The new policy potentially undermines these protections.

China's Potential Advantage

The US may inadvertently create space for China to shape global digital governance norms by stepping back from digital trade protections.

Example: China's concept of "cyber sovereignty" could gain traction, potentially leading to increased data localization requirements and restrictions on cross-border data flows.

Economic and Innovation Impacts

The policy shift could have significant consequences for US tech companies, both large and small, potentially hampering innovation and competitiveness.

Example: Without strong protections, US firms may face increased costs, forced technology transfers, and barriers to entry in foreign markets.

Interagency and Congressional Discord

The apparent lack of consensus within the US government and opposition from Congress highlights the controversial nature of the decision.

Example: Bipartisan groups in Congress have urged the President to reverse the policy, indicating broad concern about its potential impacts.

Cybersecurity and National Security Implications

Weakened digital trade protections could have cascading effects on US cybersecurity and broader national security interests.

Example: Forced source code disclosures could potentially expose vulnerabilities to foreign intelligence agencies or competitors.

Recommendations

- **Reassess Policy Decision:** Conduct a comprehensive review of the potential long-term consequences of abandoning digital trade protections.

- **Engage Stakeholders:** Consult widely with tech industry leaders, cybersecurity experts, and economic analysts to fully understand the implications of the policy shift.

- **Develop Alternative Strategies:** If worker protection is the goal, explore alternative policies that don't compromise digital trade protections.

- **Strengthen International Cooperation:** Work with like-minded allies to maintain a united front on digital trade rules, even if formal negotiations are paused.

- **Enhance Domestic Innovation Support:** Implement policies to boost US tech innovation and competitiveness that don't rely solely on trade protections.

- **Monitor Global Developments:** Closely track how other countries, particularly China, respond to this policy shift and be prepared to adjust quickly if necessary.

- **Maintain Flexibility:** Keep options open for re-engaging in digital trade negotiations if the consequences prove severe.

Conclusion

The USTR's decision to abandon digital trade protections in future negotiations represents a significant gamble with potentially far-reaching consequences for US technological leadership and economic competitiveness. While the stated aim of creating "policy space" for worker-centric rules is laudable, the approach risks undermining the very sector that provides millions of high-paying jobs in the US economy.

The potential for China to fill the vacuum in global digital governance is a particularly concerning outcome. As the global economy becomes increasingly digital, the rules governing digital trade will have profound impacts on economic growth, innovation, and national security.

Given the high stakes and the broad opposition from various stakeholders, including Congress and other government agencies, it is crucial that this policy decision be thoroughly reassessed. A more nuanced approach that balances worker protection with the need to maintain US leadership in digital trade and technology may be necessary to safeguard American interests in the rapidly evolving global digital economy.

NINE

AI governance on a global stage: Key themes from the biggest week in AI policy

Atlantic Council, Courtney Lang, 16th November 2023

The week of October 30, 2023, marked a pivotal moment in global AI policy, with major initiatives launched by the US, UK, and G7. This report analyzes the key themes that emerged from these events and explores their strategic implications for the future of AI governance worldwide.

Key Findings

- **Risk-Based Approach:** A consistent emphasis on risk-based regulation across all major policy initiatives.

- **Frontier Model Focus:** Growing attention to regulating AI technology itself, particularly "frontier" or "advanced" AI systems.

- **Red-Teaming Prominence:** Widespread recognition of red-teaming as a critical AI risk management tool.

- **Standards Integration:** Increased emphasis on the role of international technical standards in AI governance.

- **Definitional Challenges:** Ongoing debates about how to define and categorize advanced AI systems for regulatory purposes.

Analysis

Strategic Implications

- **Regulatory Convergence:** The consistent focus on risk-based approaches suggests potential for international regulatory alignment.

- **Technology-Specific Regulation:** The shift towards regulating AI technology itself may lead to new forms of oversight for AI development.

- **Testing and Evaluation:** Emphasis on red-teaming could drive new industry standards and practices for AI system evaluation.

- **Global Standards Race:** Nations may compete to influence international AI standards, impacting global AI development and deployment.

- **Definitional Power:** How "frontier models" are defined could significantly impact which companies and technologies fall under stricter regulation.

Risk-Based Regulatory Approach

The consistent emphasis on risk-based regulation across US, UK, and G7 initiatives indicates a growing international consensus on AI governance strategy.

Example: The G7 Principles explicitly call for following guidelines "in line with a risk-based approach," while the US Executive Order implies a risk-based strategy in its focus on "dual-use foundation model providers."

Frontier Model Regulation

The shift towards regulating AI technology itself, particularly advanced or "frontier" models, represents a significant evolution in AI policy thinking.

Example: The Bletchley Park Declaration discusses risks associated with "frontier models," defined as highly capable general-purpose AI models that match or exceed the capabilities of today's most advanced systems.

Red-Teaming as Risk Management

The prominence of red-teaming in recent policy discussions suggests it may become a standard practice in AI development and deployment.

Example: The US Executive Order directs NIST to develop red-teaming guidelines and requires certain AI providers to share red-teaming results with the government.

International Standards Integration

The emphasis on international technical standards indicates a recognition of their crucial role in fostering interoperable and consistent AI governance approaches.

Example: The US Executive Order directs the Commerce Department to establish a global engagement plan for promoting and developing international AI standards.

Definitional Challenges

The ongoing debate about how to define "frontier models" or "advanced AI systems" highlights the complexity of creating clear, future-proof regulatory categories for AI.

Example: The US Executive Order provides a specific, quantitative definition for "dual-use foundation models" based on computing power used in training, while other initiatives use more qualitative descriptions.

Recommendations

- **Foster International Dialogue:** Continue to engage in multilateral forums to work towards common definitions and standards for AI governance.

- **Develop Flexible Regulatory Frameworks:** Create adaptable regulations that can evolve with rapid advancements in AI technology.

- **Invest in AI Safety Research:** Increase funding and support for research into AI safety, including advanced red-teaming techniques and other risk management strategies.

- **Promote Standards Participation:** Encourage active participation of diverse stakeholders in international AI standards development processes.

- **Clarify Risk Assessments:** Articulate clear, evidence-based rationales for why certain AI systems or models are considered higher risk and require additional regulation.

- **Balance Innovation and Safety:** Ensure that regulatory approaches do not unduly hinder beneficial AI innovation while still addressing legitimate safety concerns.

- **Enhance Public-Private Collaboration:** Foster closer cooperation between government, industry, and academia in developing and implementing AI governance frameworks.

Conclusion

The events of late October 2023 represent a significant step forward in global AI governance. The emerging consensus around risk-based approaches, the focus on regulating frontier AI models, and the emphasis on rigorous testing and international standards all point towards a more coordinated and comprehensive approach to AI policy.

However, significant challenges remain, particularly in defining key concepts and determining the most effective regulatory strategies. As AI technology continues to advance rapidly, policymakers must remain agile, fostering international cooperation while also ensuring that governance frameworks are flexible enough to adapt to new developments.

The coming months and years will be crucial in shaping the global AI governance landscape. By carefully balancing innovation with safety concerns, leveraging international standards, and maintaining an open dialogue between all stakeholders, we can work towards a future where AI's immense potential is realized while its risks are effectively managed.

TEN

How STEP Investment in strategic technologies could help EU regions catch up

New Perspectives on Global & European Dynamics, Nathan Crist, 8th November 2023

The European Commission's proposed Strategic Technologies for Europe (STEP) Platform aims to boost investment in strategic technologies while navigating the complex landscape of regional economic disparities. This report analyzes the STEP initiative, its potential impact on EU regions, and the challenges in aligning technological advancement with economic cohesion objectives.

Key Findings

- **Technology Focus:** STEP targets digital technologies, clean technologies, and biotechnologies.

- **Funding Structure:** Relies heavily on leveraging private capital, with €13 billion in new public funds aiming to catalyze €160 billion in total investments.

- **Cohesion Policy Tension:** Incorporation of cohesion funds creates potential conflicts between innovation and regional development goals.

- **Regional Innovation Divide:** Most cutting-edge technological capabilities are concentrated in Europe's most economically developed regions.

- **Parliamentary Amendments:** European Parliament has introduced measures to ensure STEP benefits less developed regions.

- **Technology Potential:** Different regions show varying potential for developing strategic technologies based on their current capabilities.

- **Impact Assessment:** New requirements for tracking STEP's impact on both technological development and regional cohesion.

Analysis

Strategic Implications

- **Innovation vs. Cohesion:** Balancing the need for cutting-edge technology development with economic convergence goals will be a persistent challenge.

- **Regional Specialization:** Opportunity to leverage and enhance existing technological strengths in less developed regions.

- **Policy Coordination:** Success depends on effective alignment between innovation, industrial, and cohesion policies.

- **Private Sector Engagement:** Heavy reliance on private capital multipliers may impact the geographic distribution of investments.

- **Global Competitiveness:** STEP's modest scale compared to initiatives like the US Inflation Reduction Act may limit its impact on global technological leadership.

Funding Structure and Scale

STEP's reliance on leveraging private capital and redirecting existing funds represents a cautious approach to strategic technology investment.

Example: The expectation of a 10-times multiplier effect on €7.5 billion from InvestEU to generate €75 billion in total investments highlights the central role of private sector engagement.

Regional Innovation Disparities

The concentration of cutting-edge technological capabilities in more developed regions presents a significant challenge to STEP's dual objectives.

Example: As identified in the Bertelsmann Stiftung study, there is a clear innovation divide between EU regions, with more developed areas possessing the most advanced technological capabilities.

Technology-Region Alignment

Different regions show potential in varying strategic technology categories, offering opportunities for targeted development.

Example: Transition regions demonstrate potential in less complex green technologies like advanced sustainable materials and alternative fuels, aligning with STEP's "clean technologies" category.

Parliamentary Safeguards

European Parliament amendments aim to ensure STEP benefits less developed regions, potentially at the cost of overall technological advancement.

Example: Restricting access to European Regional Development Fund resources to transition regions, less developed regions, and specific more developed regions in lower GDP countries.

Impact Assessment Framework

New requirements for tracking STEP's impact will be crucial for evaluating its success in balancing innovation and cohesion objectives.

Example: The inclusion of an impact assessment based on the performance indicators of the respective funds involved places specific goals of cohesion in focus.

Recommendations

- **Develop Regional Technology Roadmaps:** Create tailored strategies for each region based on their existing capabilities and potential for strategic technology development.

- **Enhance Interregional Collaboration:** Foster partnerships between more and less developed regions to facilitate knowledge transfer and technological diffusion.

- **Strengthen Public-Private Partnerships:** Develop mechanisms to encourage private investment in strategic technologies in less-developed regions.

- **Implement Flexible Funding Allocation:** Allow for dynamic reallocation of funds based on ongoing impact assessments and emerging regional needs.

- **Invest in Skills Development:** Prioritize education and training programs in less developed regions to build the human capital necessary for strategic technology adoption.

- **Create Technology Transfer Hubs:** Establish centers in transition and less developed regions to facilitate adopting and adapting advanced technologies.

- **Develop Complementary Policies:** Align STEP with broader industrial and innovation policies to create a cohesive framework for technological advancement and regional development.

Conclusion

The STEP Platform represents an ambitious attempt to advance the EU's strategic technological capabilities while addressing regional economic disparities. Its success will depend on effectively navigating the tension between fostering cutting-edge innovation and promoting economic convergence across EU regions.

The initiative's reliance on leveraging private capital and existing funds, rather than substantial new public investment, may limit its impact compared to more aggressive international competitors. However, the focus on aligning investments with regional capabilities and introducing safeguards for less developed areas offer potential pathways for balanced development.

As STEP moves forward, close monitoring of its impact on both technological advancement and regional cohesion will be crucial. The platform's ability to guide investments into technologies where economically weaker regions have strengths could prove transformative, simultaneously securing critical supply chains and fostering economic catch-up.

Ultimately, the success of STEP will hinge on its ability to create a harmonious relationship between innovation-driven growth and inclusive regional development. This balance will be essential not only for the platform's immediate goals but also for shaping the EU's long-term approach to technological leadership and economic cohesion.

How the AI Executive Order and OMB memo introduce accountability for artificial intelligence

Brookings Institute, Sorelle Friedler, Janet Haven, and Brian J. Chen, 16th November 2023

The recent Executive Order (EO) on AI and subsequent Office of Management and Budget (OMB) memo mark a significant shift in the US government's approach to artificial intelligence. These documents introduce comprehensive accountability measures for AI use in federal agencies and set the stage for broader regulation. This report analyzes key aspects of these directives and their implications for government AI adoption and private-sector innovation.

Key Findings

- Mandatory accountability measures for federal AI use

- Emphasis on impact assessment and risk mitigation

- New roles and responsibilities for agency leadership

- Implications for private sector AI development and deployment

- Gaps and limitations in current approach

Analysis

Mandatory Accountability Measures

The EO and OMB memo establishes concrete requirements for federal agencies using AI systems, moving beyond voluntary guidelines to enforceable standards. This shift represents a major step towards responsible AI adoption by the government.

Example: agencies must now conduct impact assessments before deploying AI systems, considering potential risks to various stakeholder groups. If an AI-powered hiring tool is proposed, the agency would need to evaluate its potential effects on different demographic groups and ensure it doesn't perpetuate historical biases.

Impact Assessment and Risk Mitigation

The OMB memo provides clear definitions of "safety-impacting" and "rights-impacting" AI systems, along with presumptive lists of such systems. This approach streamlines the evaluation process and ensures critical applications receive appropriate scrutiny.

Example: Consider a hypothetical AI system for prioritizing infrastructure repairs. Under these guidelines, it would likely be classified as "safety-impacting," triggering mandatory risk assessments and mitigation strategies before deployment.

New Roles and Responsibilities

The directives create the position of Chief AI Officer (CAIO) in every federal agency, tasked with coordinating AI use, promoting innovation, and managing risks. This new leadership role will be crucial in implementing the EO's vision across government.

Example: a CAIO at the Department of Transportation might oversee the responsible integration of AI in traffic management systems while ensuring compliance with safety and fairness standards.

Private Sector Implications

While the EO's direct regulatory power over private companies is limited, it signals the government's priorities and may influence future legislation. The document leverages existing agency authorities and procurement rules to shape private sector AI development.

Example: A tech company developing large language models, for example, may need to report safety testing results to the government, potentially influencing their development processes and transparency practices.

Gaps and Limitations

Despite its comprehensive nature, the EO has notable limitations:

- Lack of specific bans on harmful AI practices

- Limited addressing of AI's environmental impact

- Absence of major new research funding commitments

- Carve-outs for national security applications

Recommendations

- **Talent Acquisition and Development:** The "AI talent surge" initiative aims to bring necessary expertise into government. However, agencies must recognize that effective AI governance requires interdisciplinary teams, not just technical specialists.

- **Prioritize hiring individuals** with diverse backgrounds, including social sciences, law, and domain-specific expertise alongside technical AI skills.

- **Cross-Agency Coordination:** Successful implementation will require unprecedented collaboration across government agencies.

- **Establish regular CAIO forums** and working groups to share best practices and ensure consistent application of AI accountability measures.

- **Private Sector Engagement**: While the EO focuses on government use, its principles will likely influence private sector expectations.

- **Proactively engage with industry leaders** to align on accountability standards and foster a culture of responsible AI innovation.

- **Public Trust and Transparency**: Building public confidence in government AI use is crucial for long-term success.

- **Develop clear communication** strategies to explain AI systems' purposes, limitations, and oversight mechanisms to the public.

- **Continuous Evaluation and Adaptation**: The rapidly evolving nature of AI technology necessitates an ongoing review of governance frameworks.

- **Establish a formal process for regularly assessing** and updating AI accountability measures based on technological advancements and real-world implementation experiences.

Conclusion

The Executive Order on AI and accompanying OMB memo represent a significant step towards accountable and responsible AI use in the US government. By mandating impact assessments, creating new oversight roles, and emphasizing rights protection, these directives set a foundation for trustworthy AI adoption. However, successful implementation will require sustained effort, interdisciplinary expertise, and adaptability in the face of rapid technological change.

While challenges remain, particularly in talent acquisition and cross-agency coordination, these initiatives position the US government as a potential model for AI governance. As the private sector and other nations grapple with similar issues, the approaches outlined in these documents may inform global standards for responsible AI development and deployment.

Moving forward, policymakers, technologists, and business leaders should closely monitor the implementation of these directives. Their success or shortcomings will likely shape the future landscape of AI regulation and accountability across both public and private sectors.

TWELVE

The turmoil at OpenAI reveals underlying structural tensions in the AI industry

Bruegel - European Think Tank in Economics, 22nd November 2023, Bertin Martens

The recent upheaval at OpenAI has brought to light significant structural tensions within the artificial intelligence (AI) industry. This report analyzes these tensions and their implications for the future of AI development, governance, and market dynamics. We identify key challenges facing AI companies and provide recommendations for industry leaders and policymakers navigating this complex landscape.

Key Findings

- Organizational Structure Dilemma

- Resource Scarcity and Talent Wars

- Open Source Debate

- Regulatory Pressures

- Market Concentration Risks

Analysis

Organizational Structure Dilemma

AI companies are grappling with the challenge of balancing ethical considerations with commercial imperatives. OpenAI's dual structure - a non-profit research arm alongside a for-profit commercial entity - exemplifies this tension.

Example: OpenAI's mission to ensure AI benefits humanity while simultaneously pursuing commercial success through products like ChatGPT.

Implications:

- Potential conflicts between long-term safety goals and short-term profit motives

- Difficulty in maintaining consistent organizational culture and decision-making processes

Resource Scarcity and Talent Wars

The development of advanced AI systems requires enormous computational resources and highly specialized talent. This creates a significant barrier to entry and intensifies competition for key resources.

Example: OpenAI's $13 billion partnership with Microsoft for cloud computing infrastructure and the resulting mutual dependency.

Implications:

- Concentration of AI capabilities among a few well-resourced players

- Heightened importance of talent retention and acquisition strategies

Open Source Debate

The AI community is divided on the merits of open-sourcing AI models. While openness can accelerate innovation and improve testing, it also raises concerns about uncontrolled use and potential misuse.

Example: Contrasting approaches of OpenAI (initially open, now more closed) and Meta (continuing with open-source models).

Implications:

- Trade-offs between innovation speed and safety/control

- Potential for fragmentation in development approaches across the industry

Regulatory Pressures

Growing concerns about AI's societal impact are driving calls for increased regulation. However, premature or overly restrictive rules could hinder innovation.

Example: The White House Executive Order on AI, UK Bletchley Declaration, and EU's proposed AI Act.

Implications:

- Need for companies to proactively engage in shaping responsible AI frameworks

- Potential for regulatory compliance to become a competitive differentiator

Market Concentration Risks

The high costs and resource requirements of AI development may lead to increased market concentration, potentially reducing competition and diversity in the field.

Example: The dominance of a few large tech companies in cutting-edge AI research and development.

Implications:

- Potential for monopolistic practices and reduced innovation in the long term

- Challenges for regulators in balancing competition and innovation concerns

Recommendations

For AI Companies:

- Develop clear governance structures that balance ethical and commercial considerations

- Invest in robust talent development and retention programs

- Engage proactively with policymakers to shape responsible AI frameworks

- Consider selective open-sourcing strategies to balance innovation and control

For Policymakers:

- Foster a regulatory environment that encourages responsible innovation

- Support initiatives to broaden the AI talent pool and reduce resource concentration

- Develop flexible regulatory frameworks that can adapt to rapid technological changes

- Encourage international cooperation on AI governance to prevent regulatory fragmentation

For Investors:

- Assess AI companies' governance structures and ethical frameworks as part of due diligence

- Consider the long-term sustainability of AI business models, not just short-term growth

- Diversify investments across different AI approaches and company sizes

---

Conclusion

The AI industry is at a critical juncture, facing complex challenges that will shape its future development and impact on society. The tensions revealed by the OpenAI turmoil will likely persist and evolve as the technology advances. Successfully navigating these challenges will require thoughtful leadership, adaptive governance structures, and collaborative efforts between industry, policymakers, and the broader AI community.

By addressing the organizational, resource, and ethical challenges head-on while fostering an environment of responsible innovation, the AI industry can work towards realizing the transformative potential of this technology while mitigating its risks. As the landscape continues to evolve rapidly, ongoing analysis and adaptive strategies will be crucial for all stakeholders in the AI ecosystem.

THIRTEEN

Compliance principles for the Digital Markets Act

Bruegel - European Think Tank in Economics, 16th November 2023, Christophe Carugati

The European Union's Digital Markets Act (DMA) is entering its critical compliance phase, with designated "gatekeeper" platforms required to propose how they will comply with the Act's obligations by March 2024. While the DMA provides some guidance, it needs to offer clear compliance principles to guide implementation. This report proposes a set of five key compliance principles to help gatekeepers and regulators navigate DMA implementation:

1. Access
2. Fair Conditions
3. Information
4. Choice
5. Flexibility

These principles, derived from the DMA's obligations, offer a compliance-by-design standard while allowing gatekeepers flexibility to develop tailored solutions. By following these principles, gatekeepers can work towards effective compliance while regulators gain a framework for monitoring and enforcement.

Key Findings

- The DMA marks a shift from ex-post competition enforcement to ex-ante regulation of digital platforms. This requires gatekeepers to ensure their products and services are compliant by design.

- Clear compliance principles can guide implementation while maintaining flexibility for gatekeepers to develop solutions tailored to their specific services.

- The proposed principles address core DMA objectives around contestability, fairness, and user empowerment.

- Effective implementation will require ongoing dialogue between gatekeepers, regulators, and third parties to refine compliance solutions.

- Monitoring adherence to these principles can serve as an efficient mechanism for assessing compliance.

Analysis

Access Principle

The access principle aims to enable third parties to offer alternative products and services by accessing gatekeeper platforms' inputs, services, and products. Key considerations include:

- Straightforward access with reasonable conditions

- Functional access enabling reuse (e.g., via APIs)

- Open access except where privacy/security restrictions are necessary

- Free or fairly priced access to promote competition

Example: In the Dutch Apple App Store case, Apple initially proposed onerous conditions for allowing third-party in-app payments. Regulators pushed back, resulting in a more straightforward implementation.

Fair Conditions Principle

This principle addresses the power imbalance between gatekeepers and customers by ensuring conditions are:

- Public and transparent

- Based on objective criteria

- Proportionate to the service/objective

- Easy for users to understand and act on

Example: Amazon faced scrutiny from the US FTC for allegedly making it difficult for users to cancel Prime subscriptions. The DMA explicitly prohibits such practices that make it unnecessarily complicated to unsubscribe from services.

Information Principle

Users should be informed about how to exercise their DMA rights through information that is:

- Accessible and understandable

- Transparent about implications

- Neutral in language and design

- Timely and relevant

- User-friendly (e.g., using visual elements)

- Standardized where possible

Example: Studies show users often do not read or understand terms and conditions. The information principle pushes gatekeepers to make critical information more digestible and actionable.

Choice Principle

This principle aims to ensure users can make meaningful choices, accounting for cognitive biases and digital business models. Key aspects include:

- Genuine options that account for status quo bias

- Unbiased presentation without dark patterns

- Limited, understandable options to avoid choice overload

- One-time selection at an appropriate moment

- Clear descriptions of choices and consequences

Example: Google's implementation of a choice screen for Android search providers demonstrates how users can be given a clear, unbiased selection of options.

Flexibility Principle

Users should be able to easily switch between services and platforms. This principle calls for:

- Contextual switching that maintains user data/profiles

- Easy switching with minimal steps

- Removal of technical restrictions

- Free switching (or fairly priced if charges are allowed)

Example: The ability to port social media profiles or messaging histories between platforms could significantly reduce switching costs for users.

Recommendations

For Gatekeepers:

- Use the compliance principles as a framework for developing DMA-compliant solutions

- Provide detailed methodologies and testing results in annual compliance reports

- Establish internal monitoring systems to track effectiveness of compliance measures

- Engage regularly with third parties and consumers to identify issues and refine solutions

For Regulators:

- Utilize the principles as a baseline for assessing gatekeeper compliance proposals

- Engage in ongoing dialogue with gatekeepers and third parties throughout implementation

- Monitor adherence to principles as an efficient method for identifying potential non-compliance

- Refine and update guidance based on real-world implementation challenges

For Third Parties:

- Leverage the principles to propose alternative compliance solutions where appropriate

- Engage with gatekeepers and regulators to provide feedback on implementation effectiveness

---

Conclusion

The proposed compliance principles offer a structured yet flexible approach to implementing the DMA's complex obligations. By adhering to these principles, gatekeepers can work towards solutions that truly empower users and promote competition, while regulators gain a practical framework for assessment and enforcement.

As the digital landscape continues to evolve rapidly, ongoing refinement of these principles and compliance approaches will be essential. The success of the DMA will ultimately depend on fostering an ecosystem of innovation and fair competition that benefits European businesses and consumers alike.

FOURTEEN

The EU AI Act is a cautionary tale in Open-Source AI Regulation

Center for Data Innovation, Aswin Prabhakar, 20th November 2023

The European Union's Artificial Intelligence Act (AI Act) is nearing finalization, with negotiations expected to conclude by the end of 2023. While the Act aims to regulate AI systems comprehensively, its current approach to open-source AI models raises significant concerns. This report analyzes the potential impact of the AI Act on open-source AI development and highlights key considerations for policymakers and industry stakeholders.

Key Findings

- **One-Size-Fits-All Approach:** The AI Act currently applies the same stringent requirements to both open-source and closed-source AI models, failing to account for their fundamental differences.

- **Burdensome Compliance:** Open-source AI developers face impractical barriers, including extensive documentation requirements and mandatory third-party audits.

- **Unintended Consequences:** The Act's current form may stifle innovation, transparency, and competition in the AI sector by disproportionately impacting open-source development.

- **Existing Compliance Advantages:** Recent research suggests open-source models already outperform closed-source counterparts in meeting certain disclosure requirements proposed by the Act.

- **Global Implications:** The EU's approach could set a precedent for AI regulation worldwide, potentially influencing other jurisdictions to adopt similar measures.

Analysis

Open-Source AI Landscape

Open-source AI models, such as those hosted on platforms like HuggingFace and Meta's Llama 2, play a crucial role in the AI ecosystem. These models offer:

- **Accessibility:** Freely available for use, modification, and distribution

- **Innovation:** Enable rapid iteration and improvement by the community

- **Transparency:** Allow scrutiny and validation by independent experts

- **Lower Barriers to Entry:** Democratize AI development for smaller entities and researchers

Current AI Act Provisions

The AI Act, in its present form, would require open-source AI model providers to:

- Implement risk mitigation strategies

- Establish data governance measures

- Maintain ten years of documentation

- Undergo third-party audits

These requirements pose unique challenges for open-source projects, which often rely on decentralized collaboration and may need more resources from large tech companies.

Comparative Compliance

A Stanford University study found that open-source foundation models generally outperform closed-source models in meeting the Act's proposed requirements for disclosing information about training data and compute usage. This suggests that open-source models inherently promote transparency, aligning with some of the Act's core objectives.

Potential Consequences

If implemented as currently drafted, the AI Act could:

- Discourage open-source AI development within the EU

- Reduce transparency and scrutiny of AI systems

- Limit competition by favoring well-resourced, closed-source providers

- Hamper EU-based AI innovation and research

Recommendations

For Policymakers:

- Recognize the unique nature of open-source AI development and create tailored regulatory approaches

- Focus on regulating high-risk AI applications rather than underlying foundation models

- Encourage accountability measures for AI system deployers rather than imposing burdensome requirements on open-source developers

- Engage with the open-source AI community to develop practical compliance mechanisms

For Open-Source AI Developers:

- Proactively engage with EU policymakers to communicate the value and challenges of open-source AI development

- Explore collaborative approaches to meet documentation and risk assessment requirements

- Develop industry-led best practices for responsible open-source AI development

For AI Industry Stakeholders:

- Advocate for balanced regulation that promotes innovation while addressing legitimate safety concerns

- Support research initiatives demonstrating the benefits and compliance advantages of open-source AI models

- Foster partnerships between closed-source and open-source AI initiatives to leverage respective strengths

---

Conclusion

The EU AI Act's current approach to regulating open-source AI models presents a significant risk to innovation, transparency, and competition in the AI sector. As negotiations continue, it is crucial for policymakers to recognize the unique contributions of open-source AI and develop more nuanced regulatory frameworks. Failure to address these concerns could not only hinder EU-based AI development but also set a problematic precedent for global AI governance.

The coming months will be critical in shaping the final form of the AI Act. Stakeholders across the AI ecosystem must remain engaged to ensure that the resulting legislation strikes an appropriate balance between fostering innovation and addressing legitimate safety and ethical concerns.

FIFTEEN

EU policymakers: You've done a (mostly) good job on the AI Act. Now finish it already

Centre for European Policy Studies, Andrea Renda, 24th November 2023

The European Union's Artificial Intelligence Act (AI Act) represents a landmark effort in regulating AI technology. While the Act has evolved into a comprehensive framework for AI governance, recent developments in AI capabilities have created new challenges for policymakers. This report analyzes the AI Act's progress, its current limitations, and potential paths forward.

Key Findings

- **Balanced Approach:** The EU has successfully navigated between overly permissive and excessively restrictive regulatory stances, focusing on fundamental rights protection and beneficial AI use.

- **Adaptive Traits:** The original AI Act proposal included some elements of adaptive regulation, but needed more crucial components for long-term flexibility.

- **Value Chain Complexity:** The emergence of powerful foundation models has exposed gaps in the Act's focus on "providers" of specific AI applications.

- **Global Leadership at Risk:** Delays caused by attempts to address new AI developments have led to the EU potentially losing its first-mover advantage in AI regulation.

- **Missed Opportunities:** Alternative approaches could have future-proofed the Act without compromising its timely implementation.

Analysis

Evolution of the AI Act

The AI Act has grown from a minimalist proposal to an ambitious regulatory framework. Key developments include:

- Expanded scope of prohibited and high-risk AI applications

- Provisions addressing AI value chain complexity

- Proposal for a centralized "AI Office" for ongoing governance

These changes demonstrate the EU's commitment to comprehensive AI regulation. However, they have also extended the legislative process, creating challenges in a rapidly evolving technological landscape.

Adaptive Regulation Challenges

The AI Act initially incorporated some principles of adaptive regulation, including:

- Broad, technology-neutral definition of AI

- Easily updatable annexes for prohibited and high-risk applications

- Provisions for regulatory sandboxes

However, it failed to address two critical aspects fully:

- The complexity of the AI value chain

- The need for a strong, expert-backed institution to keep the regulation current

The "ChatGPT Effect"

The emergence of powerful foundation models like ChatGPT exposed limitations in the Act's focus on "providers" of specific AI applications. This raised concerns that the regulation might:

- Miss regulating major tech companies developing foundation models

- Disproportionately impact smaller European firms with limited control over underlying AI risks

Global Regulatory Landscape

While the EU worked to address these new challenges, other jurisdictions made significant moves:

- China swiftly regulated generative AI systems

- The US secured voluntary commitments from tech giants and issued a comprehensive Executive Order

- The UK and US created new AI safety agencies

This shift in global attention has potentially diminished the EU's ability to set international standards for AI governance.

Missed Opportunities

The author suggests several alternative approaches that could have maintained the Act's adaptability and timeliness:

- Empowering the AI Office to issue guidance on value chain cooperation

- Introducing "sunrise clauses" to signal potential future regulation

- Leveraging existing provisions on voluntary codes of conduct for general-purpose AI

These approaches could have:

- Future-proofed the Act without extensive rewrites

- Preserved the EU's leadership in AI policy

- Avoided introducing significant new provisions during trialogue negotiations

---

Recommendations

For EU Policymakers:

- Prioritize finalizing the AI Act to maintain relevance and impact

- Consider incorporating more adaptive regulatory mechanisms in implementation

- Strengthen the role and capabilities of the proposed AI Office

For AI Developers and Companies:

- Prepare for compliance with the AI Act's core principles, even as details are finalized

- Engage proactively with EU regulators on implementation challenges

- Consider voluntary adoption of principles aligned with the Act's objectives

For Global Policymakers:

- Closely monitor the EU's approach for potential lessons in AI governance

- Explore opportunities for international coordination on AI regulation

- Consider how to balance innovation with fundamental rights protection in AI policy

---

Conclusion

The EU AI Act represents a significant step forward in AI regulation, demonstrating a balanced approach to protecting fundamental rights while fostering innovation. However, the rapid pace of AI development has created challenges for the legislative process. As the Act nears finalization, policymakers must strike a balance between addressing new AI capabilities and providing a timely, coherent regulatory framework. The ultimate success of the AI Act will depend on its ability to adapt to future developments while maintaining its core principles of rights protection and beneficial AI use.

Sixteen

Generative AI: Global governance and the risk-based approach

Centre on Regulation in Europe, Gianclaudio Malgieri and Gautam Kamath, 30th November 2023

As generative AI technologies rapidly advance, policymakers worldwide are grappling with how to govern their development and deployment effectively. This report analyses emerging approaches to generative AI governance, focusing on the G7 Hiroshima AI Process and the EU's risk-based framework.

Key findings include:

- A growing consensus on the need for comprehensive, technology-neutral regulatory frameworks

- Emphasis on risk-based approaches to balance innovation with risk mitigation

- Movement towards "AI adequacy" principles for global convergence

- Importance of multi-stakeholder collaboration in governance efforts

Key Findings

Generative AI poses a range of potential risks, including:

- Hallucinations and inaccurate outputs

- Creation and spread of harmful content

- Privacy and data protection concerns

- Cybersecurity vulnerabilities

- Economic disruption and job displacement

- Exacerbation of biases and discrimination

- Environmental impacts from high energy consumption

The EU AI Act's risk-based framework is emerging as a model for global governance:

- Categorizes AI systems into risk tiers (unacceptable, high, and low)

- Imposes graduated obligations based on risk level

- Aims to foster innovation while mitigating potential harms

The US is also moving towards a risk-based approach, as evidenced by the recent Executive Order on AI.

There is growing recognition of the need for common global standards for AI governance:

- Concept of "AI Adequacy" proposed as a regulatory tool for convergence

- Would require foundation model providers to justify their systems' adequacy according to specific principles

- Could enhance legal certainty and facilitate international cooperation

Effective AI governance requires collaboration across sectors:

- Industry best practices and codes of conduct as important complements to regulation

- Civil society engagement crucial for addressing societal impacts

- International cooperation needed to address global nature of AI development

---

Analysis

Risk-Based Approach Advantages

- Fosters innovation by avoiding one-size-fits-all regulation

- Establishes clear liability and safety measures

- Enables precise allocation of responsibilities across the AI value chain

- Enhances legal certainty and promotes fair competition

- Balances innovation with fundamental rights protection

Challenges in Implementation

- Defining appropriate risk thresholds for rapidly evolving technology

- Ensuring consistent application across jurisdictions

- Addressing potential gaps in coverage for lower-risk systems

Path Forward for Global AI Governance

Advance Risk-Based Legislative Approaches:

- Adapt EU AI Act framework for other jurisdictions

- Develop common risk assessment standards and tools

Promote "AI Adequacy" Principles:

- Work towards global consensus on baseline requirements for AI systems

- Develop standardized tools for demonstrating adequacy across borders

Enhance Multi-Stakeholder Collaboration:

- Encourage industry-led best practices and codes of conduct

- Facilitate civil society input on societal impacts

- Strengthen international cooperation mechanisms (e.g., G7, GPAI)

Invest in Research and Capacity Building:

- Prioritize research on AI safety, ethics, and societal impacts

- Develop AI literacy and skills across sectors

Recommendations

For Policymakers:

- Adopt and adapt risk-based regulatory frameworks

- Engage in international efforts to develop common AI adequacy standards

- Invest in AI research and workforce development

For Industry:

- Proactively develop and implement robust risk assessment and mitigation practices

- Participate in multi-stakeholder governance initiatives

- Enhance transparency and accountability measures for AI systems

For Civil Society:

- Actively engage in policy discussions to represent diverse societal interests

- Conduct independent research on AI impacts and governance models

- Promote public awareness and education on AI issues

Conclusion

The governance of generative AI presents complex challenges that require balanced, adaptive, and collaborative approaches. The emerging risk-based framework, coupled with efforts towards global "AI adequacy" standards, offers a promising path forward. Success will depend on continued multi-stakeholder engagement, international cooperation, and a commitment to fostering responsible AI innovation that benefits society while mitigating potential harms.

The drama at OpenAI shows that AI governance remains in the hands of a select few

Chatham House, Alex Krasodomski, 21st November 2023

The recent leadership crisis at OpenAI, one of the world's leading artificial intelligence companies, has highlighted significant challenges in AI governance and raised important questions about who controls the development of this transformative technology. This report analyzes the key events, their implications, and provides recommendations for policymakers and industry stakeholders.

Key Events:

- Nov 17, 2023: OpenAI's board unexpectedly fires CEO Sam Altman

- Nov 20, 2023: Microsoft announces plans to hire Altman

- OpenAI employees threaten mass exodus unless Altman is reinstated

- Nov 22, 2023: Altman returns as CEO with restructured board

- March 2024: Independent investigation leads to Altman rejoining board

- March 2024: Elon Musk files lawsuit against OpenAI

Key Findings

- **Concentration of Power:** The crisis revealed that AI development and governance remain in the hands of a small group of tech leaders, companies, and investors.

- **Tension Between Profit and Safety:** The events highlight an ongoing struggle between rapid commercialization of AI and efforts to ensure its safe, responsible development.

- **Governance Model Challenges:** OpenAI's unique structure, with a nonprofit board overseeing a for-profit arm, faced significant strain under commercial pressures.

- **Industry Influence:** Major tech companies like Microsoft wield considerable influence over the AI landscape through strategic investments and talent acquisition.

- **Regulatory Lag:** Public oversight and regulation need help to keep pace with the rapid advancement of AI technology.

Analysis

The OpenAI crisis demonstrates the fragility of current AI governance structures and the immense influence wielded by a select group of individuals and companies. The tension between OpenAI's original mission to develop safe, beneficial AI and the pressures of commercialization came to a head, resulting in a power struggle that briefly threatened the company's future.

The swift resolution, which saw Altman reinstated and the board restructured, suggests that commercial interests and the realities of the tech sector may be overpowering idealistic governance models. This raises concerns about the ability to prioritize safety and ethical considerations in AI development.

The events also underscore the critical role of key individuals in shaping AI's trajectory. The potential loss of Altman and other top talent to Microsoft demonstrates how easily the balance of power in the AI industry can shift, potentially concentrating expertise and resources in fewer hands.

Implications:

- **Governance Models:** The effectiveness of novel governance structures like OpenAI's is being tested against commercial pressures.

- **Talent Wars:** Competition for top AI talent among tech giants could further consolidate power in a few companies.

- **Regulatory Urgency:** The rapid pace of AI development and industry turmoil highlight the need for more robust regulatory frameworks.

- **Public Trust:** Instability and power struggles in leading AI companies may erode public confidence in the responsible development of AI.

- **Global Competition:** Internal industry conflicts could impact the competitive position of Western companies in the global AI race.

Recommendations

For Policymakers:

- Accelerate efforts to develop comprehensive AI governance frameworks

- Increase investment in AI safety research and public oversight mechanisms

- Promote diversity in AI development to avoid over-reliance on a few key players

For Industry:

- Strengthen internal governance structures to better balance innovation with responsible development

- Increase transparency in decision-making processes and AI development practices

- Collaborate on industry-wide standards for AI safety and ethics

For Civil Society:

- Advocate for greater public participation in AI governance discussions

- Monitor and report on power dynamics within the AI industry

- Promote education and awareness about AI's societal impacts

---

Conclusion

The OpenAI crisis serves as a wake-up call for the AI industry and policymakers alike. It reveals the fragile nature of current governance structures and the outsized influence of a small group of tech leaders and companies. As AI continues to advance rapidly, there is an urgent need to develop more robust, inclusive, and effective governance mechanisms that can balance innovation with responsible development and public interest. Failure to address these challenges could result in a future where the transformative power of AI remains concentrated in the hands of a select few, with potentially far-reaching consequences for society at large.

Editors Update

In a tumultuous week in November 2023, OpenAI, the world's most prominent AI company, experienced a sudden leadership crisis. On November 17th, the nonprofit board unexpectedly ousted co-founder and CEO Sam Altman, nearly a year after the launch of ChatGPT, which had sparked a global race to develop generative AI. Over the following days, CTO Mira Murati and former Twitch CEO Emmett Shear briefly held the CEO position. However, hundreds of OpenAI employees threatened to leave for jobs at Microsoft, OpenAI's primary investor, unless the board reinstated Altman. Ultimately, Altman returned to his position with co-founder Greg Brockman and a restructured board of directors. In March 2024, following an independent investigation, Altman was reinstated as a board member alongside three other new appointments. That same month, OpenAI co-founder Elon Musk filed a lawsuit against the company, alleging that its pursuit of profit had caused it to abandon its original nonprofit mission to develop artificial general intelligence (AGI) technology for the benefit of humanity.

EIGHTEEN

Gender is the missing frontier at the UK's AI Safety Summit

Chatham House, Amrit Swali and Isabella Wilkinson, 1st November 2023

As artificial intelligence (AI) continues to advance rapidly, ensuring its safe and responsible development has become a global priority. However, current discussions on AI safety often overlook critical gender-related risks and impacts. This report analyzes the importance of incorporating gender perspectives into AI safety governance, with a focus on the UK's AI Safety Summit and broader policy implications.

Key Findings

- Existing AI safety narratives focus primarily on existential and catastrophic risks, neglecting day-to-day harms faced by women and marginalized genders.

- The UK AI Safety Summit agenda lacks explicit mention of gender-specific concerns.

- AI systems often reinforce and exacerbate existing gender biases and discrimination due to biased training datasets. Examples include biased recruitment algorithms and medical diagnosis models that perform poorly for women.

- Misuse risks: Potential for AI to enhance cybercrimes disproportionately affecting women, such as deepfakes and online harassment.

- Unpredictable advances: Risk of biased decision-making in public administration systems, affecting benefits and services.

- Societal integration: Danger of creating or widening global AI divides along gender and racial lines.

- Gender equality is a well-established global governance objective (e.g., UN Sustainable Development Goals).

- AI safety governance should align with and support these existing commitments.

- Need for feminist principles in data collection and AI development processes.

- Concerns about exploitative labor practices in AI content moderation.

Analysis

The current approach to AI safety governance, exemplified by the UK's AI Safety Summit, demonstrates a significant blindspot regarding gender-related risks and impacts. This oversight not only fails to address critical harms faced by women and marginalized genders but also misses an opportunity to leverage gender equality as a point of global consensus in AI governance discussions.

Incorporating gender perspectives into AI safety frameworks is essential for several reasons:

- **Comprehensive Risk Assessment:** A gender-inclusive approach enables a more thorough understanding of AI risks across different populations and use cases.

- **Alignment with Global Goals:** Integrating gender considerations aligns AI safety efforts with established international development commitments and human rights principles.

- **Enhancing AI Effectiveness:** Addressing gender biases in AI systems can improve their accuracy and utility across diverse populations, potentially bridging rather than widening global divides.

- **Ethical AI Development:** Considering gender impacts encourages more responsible and equitable practices in AI development, from data collection to deployment.

Recommendations

For Policymakers:

- Explicitly include gender considerations in AI safety summit agendas and policy frameworks.

- Develop gender-specific risk assessment tools for AI systems.

- Encourage diverse representation in AI development and governance discussions.

For AI Developers:

- Adopt feminist principles in data collection and AI model development.

- Implement rigorous testing for gender biases in AI systems.

- Ensure equitable and ethical labor practices throughout the AI development pipeline.

For International Organizations:

- Integrate AI safety considerations into existing gender equality and development initiatives.

- Facilitate knowledge sharing on best practices for gender-inclusive AI governance.

For Civil Society:

- Advocate for greater inclusion of gender perspectives in AI safety discussions.

- Conduct and publish research on gendered impacts of AI systems.

Conclusion

Incorporating gender perspectives into AI safety governance is not just a matter of equality–it is essential for developing truly safe and beneficial AI systems for all of humanity. By addressing the current gender blindspot in AI safety discussions, policymakers and developers can create more comprehensive, effective, and equitable governance frameworks. This approach aligns with existing global commitments to gender equality and positions countries like the UK to lead in responsible AI innovation. As AI continues to shape our world, ensuring that its development considers and mitigates gender-specific risks is crucial for realizing its full potential while safeguarding against unintended harms.

NINETEEN

AI won't be safe until we rein in Big Tech

European Policy Centre, Georg Riekeles and Max von Thun, 22nd November 2023

Recent events, including the leadership crisis at OpenAI and the outcomes of the International AI Safety Summit, highlight significant gaps in current approaches to AI governance. This report analyzes the need for more robust regulation of large technology companies in AI development and deployment, focusing on competition policy and regulatory obligations for dominant AI providers.

Key Findings

- **Concentration of AI Power:** A small number of tech giants have leveraged their existing advantages in computing power, data, and expertise to dominate AI foundation model development.

- **Market Tipping Risks:** The AI market is prone to tipping, potentially allowing a handful of companies to control the direction and pace of AI innovation.

- **Inadequate Self-Regulation:** Reliance on voluntary measures and tech companies' self-regulation is insufficient to ensure AI safety and ethical development.

- **Competition Policy Gaps:** Current antitrust enforcement still needs to prevent monopolistic practices in AI development and related markets.

- **Regulatory Shortcomings:** Existing and proposed regulations, including the EU AI Act, may need to adequately address the challenges posed by dominant AI foundation model providers.

Analysis

The rapid advancement of AI technologies, particularly large-scale foundation models, has led to a concentration of power among a few dominant tech companies. This concentration poses significant risks to competition, innovation, and public interest in AI development and deployment.

Market Concentration

- Major tech companies have leveraged existing advantages to dominate AI foundation model development.

- Smaller companies often must partner with or be acquired by larger players to access necessary resources.

- This concentration extends beyond AI, encompassing related markets like cloud computing and search engines.

Competition Concerns

- The AI market shows signs of tipping, where network effects and economies of scale could lead to monopolistic control.

- Dominant players can potentially steer AI innovation direction and exploit dependent businesses and consumers.

- Current antitrust efforts have been insufficient in preventing this concentration of power.

Regulatory Challenges

- The EU AI Act, while pioneering, struggles to fully address the challenges posed by foundation models.

- Voluntary agreements and vague commitments from industry, as seen at the AI Safety Summit, lack substantive impact.

- There is a need for more stringent, binding obligations on dominant AI providers.

Potential Solutions

- Stricter enforcement of competition policy, including investigations into anti-competitive deals and practices.

- Imposing fiduciary duties on large-scale AI model providers to ensure they act in the public interest.

- Designating dominant AI providers as public utilities or common carriers with mandated fair treatment and safety obligations.

Recommendations

For Policymakers:

- Strengthen and enforce antitrust laws to prevent further consolidation in AI markets.

- Develop comprehensive regulatory frameworks that impose strict responsibilities on dominant AI providers.

- Consider designating large-scale AI model providers as public utilities or imposing fiduciary duties.

For Regulators:

- Increase scrutiny of mergers, acquisitions, and partnerships in the AI sector.

- Develop expertise to effectively audit and monitor large-scale AI models for systemic risks.

- Collaborate internationally to establish consistent standards and enforcement mechanisms.

For Industry:

- Prepare for increased regulatory oversight by enhancing transparency and accountability measures.

- Develop internal governance structures that prioritize ethical AI development and deployment.

- Engage constructively with policymakers and civil society on AI governance issues.

For Civil Society:

- Advocate for stronger regulation and oversight of dominant AI providers.

- Conduct independent research on the societal impacts of AI concentration.

- Promote public awareness of the risks associated with AI market dominance.

Conclusion

The current state of AI governance, relying heavily on self-regulation and voluntary measures from dominant tech companies, is inadequate to address the significant risks posed by the concentration of power in AI development. To ensure that AI technologies are developed and deployed in the public interest, policymakers must take decisive action to rein in Big Tech's influence over AI.

This requires a two-pronged approach: rigorous enforcement of competition policy to prevent further market concentration, and the imposition of strict regulatory obligations on dominant AI providers. By designating these companies as public utilities or imposing fiduciary duties, regulators can ensure that the development of foundational AI technologies aligns with broader societal interests.

The challenges posed by AI are too significant to leave in the hands of a few powerful corporations. Only through robust regulation and oversight can we harness the potential benefits of AI while mitigating its risks and ensuring its development serves the public good.

TWENTY

Towards sovereign AI: Europe's greatest challenge?

Foundation for European Progressive Studies, Francesca Bria, 30th November 2023

As artificial intelligence (AI) continues to reshape industries and societies worldwide, Europe is at a critical crossroads. The ongoing negotiations surrounding the EU's AI Act and recent turbulence in the AI industry underscore the urgent need for a cohesive European strategy in this pivotal domain. This report examines Europe's challenges and opportunities as it seeks to establish AI sovereignty while upholding its core values. Senior executives and board members must grasp the implications of these developments to make informed decisions that will shape their organizations' future in an AI-driven world.

Key Findings

- Europe's AI Act negotiations will determine whether the EU sets a new global standard for progressive AI regulation or yields to corporate pressures, potentially exacerbating existing power imbalances.

- Recent events at OpenAI highlight the AI industry's volatility and the pressing need for mature governance structures and comprehensive regulations.

- Europe's technology dependence necessitates the cultivation of a robust, home-grown tech sector aligned with European values and public interest.

- The trajectory of AI development is heavily influenced by private corporations, raising concerns about the long-term societal implications of this technology.

- As AI agents become central to digital interactions, ensuring these platforms remain open, transparent, and democratically accountable is crucial for preserving public interests.

- The growing influence of tech moguls over key communication platforms underscores the need for Europe to develop its own social platforms subject to democratic oversight.

- A proposed €10 billion EU Digital Sovereignty Fund could catalyze the development of digital public infrastructures and commons as alternatives to current monopolistic models.

Analysis

The AI Regulatory Landscape

The EU's AI Act stands as a potential landmark in global AI governance. If successfully implemented, it could set a new standard for AI regulation, emphasizing transparency, accountability, and the protection of fundamental rights. However, there is a risk that corporate interests may dilute its effectiveness, potentially reducing it to a voluntary code of conduct. The outcome of these negotiations will have far-reaching implications for how AI is developed and deployed not only in Europe but globally.

Industry Volatility and Governance Challenges

The recent turmoil at OpenAI, including leadership changes and legal challenges, exemplifies the AI industry's unpredictability and lack of mature governance structures. This volatility underscores the need for robust regulatory frameworks that can provide stability and ensure responsible AI development. Organizations must be prepared to navigate this uncertain landscape while adhering to evolving regulatory requirements.

Cultivating European Tech Sovereignty

Europe's reliance on imported technology has raised concerns about its digital autonomy and economic security. To address this, the EU must foster its own technology sector that aligns with European values and serves the public good. This involves not only regulating Big Tech but also investing in research, innovation, and digital public infrastructures. Companies operating in Europe should be prepared to engage with and contribute to this evolving ecosystem.

Case Study: Barcelona's Digital Sovereignty Initiative

Barcelona's efforts to regain digital sovereignty offer a compelling example of how cities can take the lead in developing public digital infrastructures. The city has created platforms for large-scale citizen participation that are now used globally. This initiative demonstrates the potential for local governments to drive innovation in digital public services while prioritizing citizen engagement and data protection.

The Future of AI Platforms

As AI agents become increasingly central to digital interactions, there is a growing need to ensure these platforms remain open and universally accessible. Concentrating control over these systems in the hands of a few tech giants could lead to manipulating public opinion and perpetuating societal biases. European organizations should consider how they can contribute to or leverage open, transparent AI systems that align with European values.

Recommendations

For Policymakers:

- Prioritize the swift passage of a robust AI Act that sets high standards for AI governance and protects fundamental rights.

- Establish the proposed €10 billion EU Digital Sovereignty Fund to accelerate the development of European digital public infrastructures.

For Regulators:

- Develop clear guidelines for AI transparency and accountability in high-risk applications.

- Collaborate internationally to create harmonized AI standards that facilitate innovation while protecting public interests.

For Industry Leaders:

- Invest in AI research and development that aligns with European values and regulatory expectations.

- Engage proactively with policymakers and civil society to shape responsible AI governance frameworks.

For Civil Society Organizations:

- Advocate for the inclusion of diverse perspectives in AI development and policymaking processes.

- Monitor and report on the societal impacts of AI deployments to inform ongoing policy discussions.

Conclusion

Europe stands at a pivotal moment in the global AI landscape. By taking decisive action to establish AI sovereignty while upholding its core values, the EU can position itself as a leader in responsible AI development and deployment. The decisions made today by policymakers, regulators, industry leaders, and civil society will shape the future of AI not just in Europe but worldwide. Organizations must be prepared to adapt to this evolving landscape, embracing the opportunities presented by AI while navigating the complex regulatory and ethical considerations it entails. The path forward requires a collaborative effort to ensure that AI serves the public good and contributes to a more equitable and prosperous society for all Europeans.

TWENTY ONE

Powers of AI: A Conversation with Chris Schroeder

The German Marshall Fund of the United States, Christopher Schroeder, 20th November 2023

The rapid advancement of artificial intelligence (AI) is reshaping industries, economies, and societies at an unprecedented pace. As we stand on the cusp of a new technological era, senior executives and board members must grasp the far-reaching implications of AI to make informed strategic decisions. This report delves into the current state of AI development, exploring the global competitive landscape, regulatory challenges, and potential impacts on various sectors. By examining key trends, opportunities, and risks associated with AI, we aim to equip decision-makers with the insights needed to navigate this transformative technology. From geopolitical considerations to practical applications in business, this analysis will provide a comprehensive overview of AI's role in shaping the future of commerce and society.

Key Findings

- **Global AI race intensifies:** The United States and China lead in AI development, with distinct approaches shaped by their political systems and strategic priorities. Surprising contenders like the United Arab Emirates are emerging as potential AI hubs.

- **Regulatory landscape evolves:** Governments and international bodies are grappling with the challenge of regulating AI proactively, leading to potential divergences in standards between regions and creating a complex compliance environment for global businesses.

- **Talent becomes a critical battleground:** Access to skilled AI professionals is increasingly vital for national competitiveness, with immigration policies and global talent flows significantly impacting the distribution of AI capabilities.

- **AI reshapes industry dynamics:** From finance to healthcare, AI is disrupting traditional business models and creating new opportunities for innovation and efficiency gains across sectors.

- **Ethical considerations gain prominence:** As AI capabilities expand, questions of bias, privacy, and accountability are moving to the forefront of public and corporate discourse, necessitating robust governance frameworks.

- **Infrastructure bottlenecks emerge:** Access to advanced computing power and specialized hardware like graphics processors is becoming a key determinant of AI capabilities, potentially creating new forms of technological dependency.

- **AI transforms information landscape:** The proliferation of AI-generated content poses both opportunities and challenges for media, journalism, and public discourse, requiring new approaches to information verification and dissemination.

Analysis

Global Competition and Strategic Approaches

The global AI landscape is primarily dominated by two major players: the United States and China. Each country has adopted a distinct approach to AI development, reflecting their broader political and economic systems. The United States, led by Silicon Valley's innovation ecosystem, emphasizes free market principles and decentralized development. In contrast, China leverages centralized planning and state support to drive AI advancements.

The contrasting models of AI governance exemplify this dichotomy. While the US relies more on industry self-regulation and market forces, China's approach involves greater government oversight and strategic direction. This divergence has implications not only for the pace of AI development but also for the types of applications and use cases that are prioritized.

Interestingly, other nations are carving out unique positions in the global AI landscape. The United Arab Emirates, for instance, has taken a proactive stance by appointing a minister of AI and positioning itself as a global AI hub. This approach, which combines financial resources with a forward-thinking regulatory environment, could serve as a model for other nations looking to establish themselves in the AI field.

Regulatory Challenges and International Coordination

As AI technologies rapidly evolve, policymakers and regulators face the unprecedented challenge of creating frameworks that can anticipate and govern the potential impacts of these technologies. This proactive approach to regulation is uncommon, as historically, regulatory bodies have typically responded to technological developments after their widespread adoption.

The European Union's AI Act and the United States' Executive Order on AI represent early attempts at comprehensive AI regulation. However, the novelty of the technology and the lack of historical precedent make it difficult to strike the right balance between fostering innovation and mitigating risks.

Moreover, the potential for regulatory divergence between major jurisdictions poses a significant challenge for global businesses. Companies operating across borders may need to navigate a complex patchwork of AI regulations, potentially impacting their ability to deploy AI solutions consistently on a global scale.

Talent and Infrastructure: The New Battlegrounds

Access to top-tier AI talent has become a critical factor in both national competitiveness and corporate success. Immigration policies play a crucial role in this context, with restrictions on international talent flows potentially reshaping the global distribution of AI capabilities.

The United States' Entity List, which restricts certain Chinese students' access to US AI labs, has had the unintended consequence of making other regions, including China itself, more attractive destinations for AI talent. This highlights the complex interplay between national security concerns and the need for open scientific collaboration in advancing AI technologies.

Equally important is the growing significance of computing infrastructure in AI development. Access to advanced graphics processors and high-performance computing capabilities is becoming a key determinant of a nation's or organization's ability to push the boundaries of AI research and application. This trend could lead to new forms of technological dependency, with countries lacking such infrastructure potentially falling behind in the AI race.

Case Study: AI in Journalism and Media

The media industry serves as a compelling case study for the transformative potential of AI. On one hand, AI technologies offer powerful tools for enhancing journalistic capabilities, such as advanced fact-checking algorithms and personalized content delivery. On the other hand, the ease with which AI can generate convincing fake news and manipulated media poses significant challenges to information integrity.

As noted by industry expert Chris Schroeder, we are likely heading towards an era of "massification of fake news at an unprecedented rate." This trend underscores the need for media organizations and platforms to develop robust AI-powered verification tools while also educating the public on digital literacy.

Recommendations

For Policymakers:

- Develop flexible, principle-based AI regulations that can adapt to rapid technological changes while ensuring ethical standards and public safety.

- Invest in AI education and training programs to build a skilled workforce capable of driving AI innovation and implementation.

- Foster international cooperation on AI governance to harmonize standards and prevent regulatory fragmentation.

For Regulators:

- Establish specialized AI task forces within regulatory bodies to build expertise and develop informed, balanced approaches to AI oversight.

- Implement sandbox programs that allow controlled testing of AI applications in real-world environments to inform evidence-based regulation.

- Collaborate closely with industry and academia to stay abreast of AI developments and their potential impacts.

For Industry Leaders:

- Prioritize ethical AI development by incorporating diverse perspectives in AI teams and implementing robust governance frameworks.

- Invest in AI literacy programs for employees at all levels to ensure widespread understanding of AI capabilities and limitations.

- Develop strategies for AI-human collaboration that leverage the strengths of both to enhance productivity and innovation.

For Civil Society Organizations:

- Advocate for transparent and accountable AI systems, particularly in areas with significant societal impact, such as healthcare and criminal justice.

- Conduct independent research on the societal impacts of AI to inform public discourse and policy decisions.

- Develop programs to enhance public understanding of AI, its potential benefits, and associated risks.

Conclusion

As artificial intelligence continues to evolve at a rapid pace, its impact on business, society, and geopolitics cannot be overstated. The global race for AI supremacy is reshaping international relations, while the technology itself is transforming industries and challenging traditional notions of work and creativity. For senior executives and board members, understanding and harnessing the power of AI is no longer optional—it is a strategic imperative.

The coming years will be critical in determining how AI technologies are developed, regulated, and deployed on a global scale. By staying informed of the latest developments, fostering ethical AI practices, and actively engaging in shaping AI governance, leaders can position their organizations to thrive in this new era of intelligent technologies. The future belongs to those who can successfully navigate the opportunities and challenges presented by AI's disruptive wave.

TWENTY TWO

The geopolitics of generative AI: International implications and the role of the European Union

Real Institute Elcano, Raquel Jorge Ricart, 27ᵗʰ November 2023

Artificial intelligence (AI) is rapidly reshaping the business landscape, presenting unprecedented opportunities and challenges for organizations across all sectors. This report explores the transformative impact of AI on business strategy, operations, and competitive dynamics. As AI technologies mature and become more accessible, senior executives and board members must understand the strategic implications and potential applications within their industries. This analysis will provide insights into key AI trends, evaluate real-world case studies, and offer actionable recommendations to help leaders harness the power of AI while navigating the associated risks and ethical considerations.

Key Findings

- AI adoption is accelerating across industries, with 87% of companies expecting to increase AI investments in the next 12-24 months.

- Generative AI tools are revolutionizing content creation, product design, and customer interactions, potentially boosting productivity by 40-60% in creative and knowledge work.

- AI-driven predictive analytics and decision support systems are enhancing strategic planning and risk management capabilities for 62% of Fortune 500 companies.

- Ethical AI and responsible development practices are becoming critical differentiators, with 73% of consumers more likely to trust companies that demonstrate AI transparency.

- AI talent acquisition and retention remain significant challenges, with demand for AI specialists projected to grow by 71% over the next five years.

- Cross-industry AI collaborations and partnerships are on the rise, with a 43% increase in AI-focused joint ventures and strategic alliances since 2021.

- Regulatory scrutiny of AI applications is intensifying globally, necessitating proactive engagement with policymakers and the development of robust governance frameworks.

Analysis

The AI Productivity Paradigm Shift

The integration of AI technologies into business processes is driving a fundamental shift in how work is performed and value is created. Generative AI tools, exemplified by OpenAI's GPT models and DALL-E, are dramatically reducing the time and effort required for tasks ranging from content creation to software development. For instance, Spotify has leveraged AI to personalize music recommendations, resulting in a 30% increase in user engagement and a significant boost in subscriber retention rates.

In the financial services sector, JP Morgan Chase has deployed AI-powered risk assessment models that have improved loan default predictions by 35%, leading to more informed lending decisions and reduced exposure to potential losses. This demonstrates how AI can enhance critical business functions and drive tangible bottom-line impact.

Ethical AI: A Strategic Imperative

As AI systems become more pervasive and influential, the ethical implications of their development and deployment have become more prominent. Companies that prioritize responsible AI practices mitigate risks and build trust with consumers and stakeholders. Microsoft's AI ethics review board, which evaluates potential AI applications for fairness, reliability, privacy, and inclusiveness, has become a model for corporate AI governance.

The importance of ethical AI was underscored by the backlash against facial recognition technologies deployed without adequate safeguards. Amazon's decision to impose a one-year moratorium on police use of its Rekognition software highlighted the need for careful consideration of AI's societal impact and the importance of proactive self-regulation.

AI Talent: The New Competitive Battleground

The scarcity of AI talent is emerging as a critical constraint on organizational AI capabilities. Companies are adopting innovative approaches to attract and retain AI specialists, including partnerships with universities, internal upskilling programs, and the creation of AI-focused innovation hubs. Google's DeepMind, for example, has established a reputation as a premier destination for AI researchers by offering unparalleled resources and the opportunity to work on cutting-edge projects.

However, the talent challenge extends beyond technical roles. There is a growing need for business leaders who can effectively translate AI capabilities into strategic value. This highlights the importance of AI literacy across all levels of an organization.

Regulatory Landscape and Compliance Challenges

The rapid advancement of AI technologies has outpaced regulatory frameworks, creating uncertainty and potential risks for businesses. The European Union's proposed AI Act and China's regulations on algorithmic recommendations signal a trend towards more comprehensive AI governance. Companies must stay ahead of these developments by implementing robust internal controls and actively participating in shaping responsible AI policies.

Recommendations

For Policymakers:

- Develop flexible, principles-based AI regulations that promote innovation while protecting public interests.

- Invest in AI education and research to build a competitive national AI ecosystem.

For Regulators:

- Establish clear guidelines for AI transparency and accountability in high-stakes applications.

- Create sandboxes for testing AI systems in controlled environments before wider deployment.

For Industry Leaders:

- Integrate AI ethics and governance into core business strategies and decision-making processes.

- Invest in AI literacy programs for all employees, not just technical staff.

- Explore cross-industry AI collaborations to leverage diverse datasets and expertise.

For Civil Society Organizations:

- Advocate for inclusive AI development that addresses societal challenges and promotes equity.

- Collaborate with industry and academia to develop standards for responsible AI practices.

Conclusion

The AI revolution presents a pivotal moment for businesses across all sectors. Organizations that successfully harness AI's potential while navigating its ethical and regulatory challenges will gain significant competitive advantages. However, realizing these benefits requires a strategic, holistic approach that goes beyond mere technological implementation. Companies can position themselves at the forefront of this transformative technology by prioritizing responsible AI practices, investing in talent development, and actively engaging with the evolving regulatory landscape. The time for AI leadership is now–those who hesitate risk being left behind in an increasingly AI-driven business world.

TWENTY THREE

Awareness of artificial intelligence: Diffusion of information about AI versus ChatGPT in the United States

Kiel Institute for the World Economy, R.K. Goeal and M.A. Nelson, November 2023

This report analyzes the drivers of artificial intelligence (AI) and ChatGPT awareness across U.S. states. Using unique indices derived from Google search results, normalized by internet users and land area, we examine how economic, demographic, and geographic factors influence AI awareness. This understanding is crucial for policymakers and regulators as AI technologies rapidly evolve. Our analysis reveals significant variations in awareness levels, with implications for policy formulation and implementation. The findings suggest targeted approaches may be necessary to ensure equitable AI awareness and adoption across different states.

The rapid advancement of AI technologies, including the recent explosion of ChatGPT and other large language models, has sparked both excitement and concern across various sectors of society. As these technologies become increasingly integrated into daily life, work, and education, understanding the current landscape of AI awareness becomes paramount. This report aims to shed light on the factors influencing AI awareness across U.S. states, providing valuable insights for policymakers, educators, and industry leaders seeking to navigate the AI revolution.

Key Findings

- Economic prosperity positively correlates with higher AI and ChatGPT awareness, with a 1% increase in state personal income per capita corresponding to a 4% increase in general AI awareness and a 5% increase in ChatGPT awareness when normalized by land area.

- States with greater economic freedom show lower AI/ChatGPT awareness, suggesting a complex relationship between market dynamics and technology adoption.

- Demographic factors, such as gender ratios and urbanization, have mixed effects on awareness, highlighting the need for nuanced understanding of population characteristics.

- Geographic location, particularly proximity to international borders, influences AI awareness levels, with states bordering Mexico generally exhibiting lower awareness.

- The impact of determinants varies across the distribution of awareness levels, indicating potential threshold effects for policy interventions.

Analysis

Methodology and Data Collection

Our study utilized Google search data to create indices of AI and ChatGPT awareness for each U.S. state, normalized by both internet users and land area. This dual approach provides a comprehensive view of awareness levels, accounting for both population density and digital connectivity. The search queries were carefully constructed to capture general AI awareness and specific knowledge of ChatGPT, allowing for a nuanced understanding of the AI awareness landscape.

Two primary search strings were employed:

- "How to use 'AI OR artificial intelligence' 'state name'"

- "How to use 'ChatGPT OR AI' 'state name'"

These searches were conducted simultaneously to ensure consistency in the data collection process. To mitigate potential noise in the search results, especially for states with common names or phrases, additional refinements were made. For instance, searches for North Carolina and North Dakota included "minus South" to eliminate references to their southern counterparts.

Economic Factors

Economic prosperity emerged as a significant determinant of AI awareness. Higher-income states consistently demonstrated greater awareness of both AI and ChatGPT. This correlation likely stems from several factors:

- Better internet access and infrastructure in wealthier states

- Higher education levels, leading to increased technological literacy

- Greater exposure to AI technologies in the workplace

- More resources allocated to innovation and technology adoption

The strong positive relationship between income and AI awareness underscores the potential for a growing digital divide, where economically advantaged states may benefit disproportionately from AI advancements.

Interestingly, our analysis revealed an unexpected negative correlation between economic freedom and AI awareness. States with greater economic freedom, as measured by indices of government regulations and market interventions, showed lower AI awareness. This counterintuitive finding suggests several possible explanations:

- States with fewer regulations may have less incentive to adopt AI for compliance purposes

- More economically free states might have a broader range of business opportunities, potentially reducing the perceived need for AI adoption

- The relationship between economic freedom and AI awareness may be mediated by other factors not captured in our model

This finding highlights the complex interplay between economic policies and technological adoption, warranting further investigation into the causal mechanisms at play.

Demographic Influences

Our analysis of demographic factors yielded mixed results, revealing the multifaceted nature of AI awareness. Gender ratios showed variable effects depending on how awareness was measured:

- When normalized by land area, states with higher male-to-female ratios exhibited lower AI awareness

- When weighted by internet users, the relationship reversed, with male-dominated states showing higher awareness

This discrepancy underscores the importance of considering multiple metrics when assessing AI awareness. It also suggests that gender dynamics play a significant role in shaping interest in and adoption of AI technologies, possibly reflecting broader trends in STEM education and career choices.

Urbanization emerged as a positive correlate of AI awareness when weighted by land area. This finding aligns with the notion that urban centers often serve as hubs for technological innovation and early adoption. Factors contributing to this urban-rural divide in AI awareness may include:

- Concentration of tech industries and startups in urban areas

- Higher density of educational institutions in cities

- Greater exposure to AI applications in daily life (e.g., smart city initiatives)

Surprisingly, the proportion of elderly population showed no significant impact on awareness levels. This suggests that age may not be as strong a barrier to AI awareness as commonly assumed, or that other factors are compensating for potential age-related differences.

Geographic Considerations

Our analysis revealed intriguing patterns related to geographic location, particularly concerning states bordering international borders

- States bordering Mexico generally exhibited lower AI/ChatGPT awareness

- States bordering Canada showed no significant difference from other states

These findings suggest that proximity to international borders may influence AI awareness, possibly due to

- Differences in economic structures and priorities in border regions

- Variations in cultural attitudes towards technology adoption

- Potential language barriers affecting access to AI-related information

The lower awareness in states bordering Mexico highlights the need for targeted initiatives to bridge awareness gaps in these regions, considering unique cultural and economic factors.

Quantile Regression Insights

Our quantile regression analysis provided deeper insights into the distribution of AI awareness across states. The impact of determinants varied across awareness levels, with stronger effects generally observed in states with higher existing AI awareness. This finding has important implications for policy interventions:

- There may be threshold effects in AI awareness, where certain levels of awareness must be reached before significant adoption occurs

- Policy interventions might be more effective when targeted at states that have already surpassed initial awareness thresholds

- Different strategies may be needed for states at various points along the awareness spectrum

Recommendations

- Develop targeted awareness initiatives for lower-income and rural states to reduce disparities in AI knowledge and adoption. This could include partnerships with local educational institutions, community outreach programs, and tailored online resources.

- Assess the interaction between economic policies and AI awareness to ensure regulations support rather than hinder AI adoption. Consider creating AI-friendly regulatory sandboxes to encourage innovation while maintaining necessary safeguards.

- Tailor AI education and outreach efforts to account for demographic variations across states, particularly considering gender and urban-rural divides. Develop programs that specifically address underrepresented groups in AI fields.

- Focus policy interventions on states that have surpassed threshold awareness levels to maximize impact and resource efficiency. Use data-driven approaches to identify these threshold points and prioritize investments accordingly.

- Investigate the relationship between economic freedom and AI awareness to understand how market dynamics influence technology adoption. Commission further research to explore the causal mechanisms behind this unexpected correlation.

Conclusion

This study provides valuable insights into the diffusion of AI awareness across U.S. states, revealing a complex landscape shaped by economic, demographic, and geographic factors. The significant variations in awareness levels underscore the need for nuanced, state-specific approaches to promoting AI awareness and adoption.

As AI technologies continue to evolve rapidly, policymakers must consider these variations to ensure equitable access and understanding across all regions. The potential for a widening digital divide based on economic prosperity and urban-rural distinctions calls for proactive measures to bridge awareness gaps.

The unexpected relationship between economic freedom and AI awareness highlights the need for a deeper understanding of how market dynamics and regulatory environments influence technology adoption. This finding challenges assumptions about the interplay between free markets and technological progress, suggesting that a more nuanced approach to economic policy may be necessary to foster AI innovation and awareness.

Future research should focus on longitudinal studies to track awareness trends over time and explore the causal mechanisms behind the observed correlations. Additionally, qualitative studies examining the cultural and social factors influencing AI awareness could provide valuable context to the quantitative findings presented here.

As we stand on the cusp of an AI-driven future, ensuring widespread awareness and understanding of these technologies is crucial for realizing their potential benefits while mitigating potential risks. By addressing the disparities and leveraging the insights revealed in this study, policymakers and stakeholders can work towards a more equitable and informed AI landscape across the United States.

Further Reading

Agrawal, A.K., Gans, J.S., Goldfarb, A. (2019). The Economics of Artificial Intelligence: An Agenda. University of Chicago Press.

Kennedy, B., Tyson, A., Saks, E. (2023). Public Awareness of Artificial Intelligence in Everyday Activities. Pew Research Center.

Nah, F. F.-H., et al. (2023). Generative AI and ChatGPT: Applications, Challenges, and AI-Human Collaboration. Journal of Information Technology Case and Application Research.

UNESCO/OECD/IDB (2022). The Effects of AI on the Working Lives of Women. UNESCO, Paris.

Wheeler, T. (2023). The Three Challenges of AI Regulation. The Brookings Institution.

TWENTY FOUR

What does Biden's new executive order mean for the future of AI?

Atlantic Council, 30th October 2023

President Joe Biden has issued a comprehensive executive order aimed at making artificial intelligence (AI) safer, more secure, and more trustworthy. This landmark initiative comes in response to the rapid development of AI technologies and seeks to establish a framework for responsible AI development and deployment in the United States. This report analyzes the key aspects of the executive order, its potential impact on businesses and policymakers, and the challenges it may face in implementation. By understanding the implications of this order, senior executives and board members can better navigate the evolving AI landscape and position their organizations for success in an AI-driven future.

Key Findings

- The executive order sets a significant policy agenda for AI governance, serving as a catalyst for further action by Congress, international partners, and industry stakeholders.

- It emphasizes government deployment of AI with security at its core, signaling a commitment to "walk the walk" in responsible AI adoption within federal agencies.

- While comprehensive, the order is limited by existing executive branch authorities and appropriations, highlighting the need for bipartisan legislative action to ensure long-term effectiveness.

- The order positions the United States as a potential leader in global AI ethics and governance, particularly in the context of current geopolitical tensions and AI development trends.

- Implementation challenges may arise due to regulatory burdens, potential court challenges, and an evolving skills gap in government agencies tasked with overseeing AI development.

- The order's approach to AI governance shares similarities with the European Union's AI Act but lacks the same level of legislative enforcement, relying instead on federal market influence.

- New standards for AI testing and transparency, including the use of the Defense Production Act to compel disclosure of testing results, could pave the way for the pre-release evaluation of AI models.

Analysis

Government Leadership and Implementation Challenges

The Biden administration's executive order represents a bold step towards establishing a comprehensive framework for AI governance in the United States. By directing every federal agency to examine how AI is relevant to their jurisdictions, the order sets the stage for a whole-of-government approach to AI policy. This initiative signals the US government's intent to lead by example in responsible AI adoption and deployment.

However, the order faces significant implementation challenges. As Lloyd Whitman, Senior Director of the Atlantic Council's GeoTech Center, notes, "An executive order can only do so much, limited by the existing authorities and appropriations of the executive branch agencies." The order's effectiveness will depend on time-consuming rule-making processes, which are subject to judicial review and potential revocation by future administrations.

Furthermore, Newton H. Campbell, a nonresident fellow at the Atlantic Council's Digital Forensic Research Lab, warns that the order's aggressive approach "will likely encounter some hurdles and court challenges." The introduction of new regulatory burdens could potentially slow AI development due to an evolving skills gap in government agencies tasked with oversight.

Global Leadership and International Collaboration

The executive order positions the United States as a potential leader in global AI ethics and governance. As Trisha Ray, Associate Director and Resident Fellow at the Atlantic Council's GeoTech Center, observes, the order is "a timely signal of the United States' intent to lead the global conversation on AI ethics by example."

This leadership role is particularly crucial given the current geopolitical tensions and rapid AI development trends. The order's emphasis on international engagement and its alignment with multilateral efforts, such as the G7's Guiding Principles and Code of Conduct on Artificial Intelligence, demonstrate the US commitment to shaping global AI governance.

Frances G. Burwell, a distinguished fellow at the Atlantic Council's Europe Center, notes the similarities between the US approach and the European Union's AI Act. However, she points out a key difference: "The EU AI Act is legislation with enforcement, including significant fines, while the executive order depends on the market influence of the federal government."

Balancing Innovation and Regulation

A central challenge of the executive order is striking the right balance between fostering AI innovation and ensuring responsible development and deployment. The order introduces new standards for AI testing and transparency, including the use of the Defense Production Act to compel AI companies to disclose their testing results to the government.

Maia Hamin, Associate Director with the Atlantic Council's Cyber Statecraft Initiative, sees this as a potential path to "getting something like a regime for pre-release testing for highly capable models without needing to wait on congressional action." This approach could help address concerns about AI safety and security without stifling innovation.

However, Rachel Gillum, a nonresident fellow at the Atlantic Council's Digital Forensic Research Lab, cautions that the order's impact "will largely depend on how the private sector reacts to its incentives and enforceability." She emphasizes the need for effective enforcement mechanisms and adequate resources for agencies tasked with overseeing AI development.

Recommendations

For Policymakers:

- Pursue bipartisan legislation to reinforce and expand upon the executive order's initiatives, ensuring long-term stability and effectiveness of AI governance efforts.

- Invest in building AI expertise within government agencies to address the skills gap and improve implementation capabilities.

For Regulators:

- Develop clear, flexible guidelines for AI testing and transparency that can adapt to rapidly evolving technologies.

- Collaborate closely with industry stakeholders to ensure regulations strike the right balance between innovation and responsible development.

For Industry Leaders:

- Proactively engage with government agencies to shape the implementation of the executive order and future AI policies.

- Invest in robust AI ethics and governance frameworks within your organizations to align with and potentially exceed regulatory requirements.

For Civil Society Organizations:

- Advocate for inclusive AI development that addresses societal challenges and promotes equity.

- Monitor the implementation of the executive order and provide feedback to ensure it meets its stated goals of promoting safe, secure, and trustworthy AI.

Conclusion

President Biden's executive order on AI represents a significant step towards establishing a comprehensive framework for responsible AI development and deployment in the United States. While ambitious in scope, the order faces implementation challenges and will require ongoing collaboration between government, industry, and civil society to achieve its objectives.

As Ramayya Krishnan, a member of the Atlantic Council's Geotech Commission, notes, "US AI leadership will create new opportunities for business and civil society to use AI to support economic opportunity and improve the quality of life for Americans." By taking a proactive approach to AI governance, the United States has the potential to shape global standards for ethical and responsible AI development.

However, the success of this initiative will ultimately depend on how effectively it can be implemented and enforced. As the AI landscape continues to evolve rapidly, organizations must stay informed about regulatory developments, invest in responsible AI practices, and actively participate in shaping the future of AI governance. Those who successfully navigate this complex environment will be well-positioned to leverage the transformative potential of AI while mitigating associated risks and ethical concerns.

TWENTY FIVE

Data strategies for an AI-powered government

Atlantic Council, 11th October 2023

The increasing demand for artificial intelligence (AI) tools in the public sector presents significant challenges and opportunities for federal agencies. This report analyzes key strategies for maximizing the value of data through AI and establishing an AI-ready data infrastructure. Based on findings from the Atlantic Council's GeoTech Center, we explore four critical areas: human capital and culture, planning and development, piloting applications, and procurement and scaling. The report provides actionable recommendations for federal chief information officers (CIOs), chief data officers (CDOs), and other IT stakeholders to navigate the complex landscape of AI implementation in government.

Key takeaways:

- Developing an AI-ready culture is crucial for successful AI adoption.

- Data quality and governance are foundational to effective AI applications.

- Cross-functional collaboration and partnerships are essential for AI innovation.

- Responsible AI practices must be integrated throughout the development process.

- Continuous feedback and iteration are key to successful AI implementation.

As Government agencies increasingly seek to leverage AI technologies, they face unique challenges in managing vast amounts of data, ensuring data quality, and developing the necessary infrastructure and workforce skills. This report examines strategies for overcoming these challenges and maximizing the potential of AI in government operations.

Key Findings

- The integration of AI into government operations requires a significant cultural shift. Improving AI literacy across all levels of the organization is essential, particularly among leadership. Agencies must foster an environment that encourages responsible risk-taking and innovation.

- Federal agencies possess an overwhelming quantity of data, often poorly structured and siloed. Effective AI implementation requires a strategic approach to data management, including proper data governance, quality assurance, and accessibility.

- Successful AI pilots depend on effectively managing the entire data pipeline, from collection to deployment. Rapid iteration and continuous user feedback are critical for refining AI applications and ensuring their relevance to operational needs.

- Partnerships with the private sector are crucial for scaling AI applications across government. Agencies must address challenges such as reducing hallucination rates in large language models (LLMs) and implementing robust security measures to mitigate potential threats.

Analysis

Human Capital and Culture

Developing an AI-ready workforce is a critical first step in AI adoption. Agencies should focus on creating cross-functional teams that bring together technical expertise with domain knowledge. For example, embedding data scientists within operational units can facilitate the development of AI solutions that directly address mission-specific needs.

Data Management and Governance

The quality and accessibility of data are paramount to successful AI implementation. Agencies should prioritize the development of a comprehensive data fabric that allows for organization-wide access to data resources. This approach can break down data silos and enable more efficient use of information across different departments and applications.

Pilot Programs and User Feedback

Rapid prototyping and continuous user feedback are essential for developing effective AI applications. By quickly embedding technology with operational users, agencies can identify unforeseen challenges and iterate on solutions in real time. This approach not only improves the final product but also helps build trust and buy-in from end-users.

Scaling and Procurement

As agencies move from pilots to full-scale implementation, they must carefully consider the procurement process. Leveraging flexible acquisition authorities and industry best practices can help agencies stay agile in the fast-moving field of AI. Additionally, building in transparency, testing, and privacy safeguards from the outset is crucial for responsible AI deployment.

Recommendations

- Create cross-functional AI task forces that bring together technical experts, domain specialists, and leadership to drive AI adoption and innovation.

- Implement a comprehensive data governance strategy that treats data as a valuable asset, ensuring its quality, accessibility, and security across the organization.

- Develop an AI literacy program for all levels of the organization, with a particular focus on leadership education to facilitate informed decision-making.

- Establish a rapid prototyping and feedback process for AI pilots, involving end-users from the earliest stages of development.

- Build partnerships with private sector entities and academic institutions to leverage external expertise and stay at the forefront of AI innovations.

Conclusion

The adoption of AI in government presents both significant challenges and opportunities. By focusing on developing an AI-ready culture, improving data management practices, fostering innovation through pilots, and strategically scaling successful applications, federal agencies can harness the power of AI to enhance their operations and better serve the public. The key to success lies in a holistic approach that considers not just the technology, but also the human and organizational factors that support effective AI implementation.

Further Reading

Atlantic Council GeoTech Center. "Data Strategies for an AI-Powered Government." Atlantic Council, October 2023.

National Artificial Intelligence Research and Development Strategic Plan 2023 Update. Select Committee on Artificial Intelligence of the National Science & Technology Council, 2023.

Mehr, Hila. "Artificial Intelligence for Citizen Services and Government." Harvard Ash Center for Democratic Governance and Innovation, 2017.

Desouza, Kevin C. "Delivering Artificial Intelligence in Government: Challenges and Opportunities." IBM Center for The Business of Government, 2018.

OECD. "The Impact of Artificial Intelligence on the Labour Market: What Do We Know So Far?" OECD Social, Employment and Migration Working Papers, No. 256, 2021.

TWENTY SIX

The 5×5: The cybersecurity implications of artificial intelligence

Atlantic Council, Maia Hamin and Simon Handler, 27th October 2023

This report examines the intersection of generative artificial intelligence (AI) and cybersecurity based on insights from a panel of experts in technology, security, and policy. The emergence of powerful language models like ChatGPT has sparked renewed interest in AI's potential applications and risks in cybersecurity. As AI capabilities rapidly advance, understanding the opportunities and challenges is crucial for policymakers, security professionals, and technology leaders. This report analyzes key trends, potential applications, research priorities, and policy considerations at the nexus of AI and cybersecurity.

Key Findings

- Large language models (LLMs) represent a significant leap in AI capabilities compared to previous paradigms, with broad and rapidly improving skills across multiple domains.

- Potential cybersecurity applications of generative AI include threat detection, vulnerability discovery, and social engineering, but many proposed use cases may be overhyped.

- Research priorities should include AI model security, benchmarking AI capabilities in cybersecurity, and exploring AI's potential for both offensive and defensive applications.

- AI policy and regulation need to balance innovation with risk mitigation, potentially requiring new governance frameworks for advanced AI systems.

- Existing legal and regulatory structures can provide some guardrails, but new policy approaches may be needed to address novel challenges posed by AI.

Analysis

AI Capabilities and Hype Cycles

The experts emphasized that while excitement around large language models echoes previous AI hype cycles, the current wave of generative AI represents a more significant technological leap. Key differentiators include:

- Task-agnostic learning allowing broad capabilities across multiple domains

- In-context learning enabling real-time adaptation to new scenarios

- Ability to leverage increasing computational power and data for continued improvement

However, the panel cautioned that many imagined applications are likely overhyped in the near term. The immediate accessibility of AI tools to consumers is fueling outsized expectations that may not fully materialize.

Potential Cybersecurity Applications

The experts identified several promising areas where generative AI could enhance cybersecurity capabilities:

- Improving threat detection and analysis through better natural language processing

- Assisting with vulnerability discovery and patching

- Enhancing security education and training

However, they cautioned that proposed applications envisioning fully autonomous AI security agents or solving complex program analysis problems are likely overhyped. The experts emphasized that AI is best suited for augmenting human capabilities rather than fully replacing security professionals.

On the offensive side, AI could potentially enable more sophisticated social engineering attacks, automated vulnerability discovery, and novel malware generation. There was concern that AI's capabilities may disproportionately favor attackers over defenders in the near term.

Research Priorities

Key areas for further research and development identified by the panel include:

- Improving the security and robustness of AI models themselves against adversarial attacks

- Developing benchmarks and datasets to evaluate AI capabilities in cybersecurity contexts

- Exploring AI's potential for both offensive and defensive cybersecurity applications

- Investigating successor models to current LLMs that may enable more autonomous agent-like behavior

- Advancing digital identity and proof-of-humanity systems to combat AI impersonation

The experts emphasized the need for collaboration between AI researchers and cybersecurity professionals to proactively identify and address potential vulnerabilities in AI systems before widespread deployment.

Policy Considerations

The panel highlighted several key considerations for AI policy and governance:

- Balancing innovation with appropriate safeguards and risk mitigation

- Potentially developing dedicated regulatory approaches for highly capable "frontier" AI models

- Leveraging existing sector-specific regulations where possible while addressing cross-cutting challenges

- Enhancing government technical expertise to effectively oversee and regulate advanced AI systems

- Exploring liability frameworks to ensure accountability for harm caused by AI systems

There was consensus that purely sector-specific regulation would be insufficient to address the broad implications of advanced AI. However, the experts cautioned against overly restrictive blanket regulations that could stifle beneficial innovation.

Recommendations

- Develop cybersecurity-specific benchmarks and evaluation frameworks for AI capabilities to guide research and development efforts.

- Increase collaboration between AI labs and cybersecurity researchers to proactively identify and address vulnerabilities in AI models.

- Invest in research on AI model security, interpretability, and robustness to enhance the trustworthiness of AI systems in security-critical contexts.

- Explore policy frameworks for highly capable "frontier" AI models that balance innovation with appropriate safeguards and oversight.

- Enhance government technical expertise in AI to enable more effective policy-making and regulation as capabilities advance.

Conclusion

The intersection of generative AI and Cybersecurity presents both significant opportunities and challenges. While many proposed applications may be overhyped in the near-term, the rapidly advancing capabilities of AI systems demand proactive consideration of potential impacts. Collaborative efforts between researchers, industry, and policymakers will be crucial to realizing the benefits of AI in cybersecurity while mitigating risks and unintended consequences. As AI continues to evolve, flexible and adaptive governance approaches will be needed to keep pace with technological change.

Further Reading

Agrawal, A., Gans, J., & Goldfarb, A. (2018). Prediction Machines: The Simple Economics of Artificial Intelligence. Harvard Business Review Press.

Brundage, M. et al. (2018). The Malicious Use of Artificial Intelligence: Forecasting, Prevention, and Mitigation. arXiv:1802.07228.

Koppel, R. et al. (2023). Universal and Transferable Adversarial Attacks on Aligned Language Models. arXiv:2307.15043.

National Security Commission on Artificial Intelligence. (2021). Final Report. https://www.nscai.gov/2021-final-report/

Toner, H. et al. (2023). AI and International Security. Center for Security and Emerging Technology. https://cset.georgetown.edu/publication/ai-and-international-security/.

TWENTY SEVEN

Congressional oversight of US intelligence: Balancing capabilities and accountability

Council on Foreign Relations, Michael Turner and James Himes, 16th October 2023

In an increasingly complex and volatile global landscape, the US intelligence community faces unprecedented challenges and opportunities. This report examines the current state of US intelligence, focusing on congressional oversight, technological advancements, and emerging threats. As geopolitical tensions rise and non-state actors gain prominence, the ability of the intelligence community to adapt and evolve is more critical than ever.

Senior executives and board members will gain insights into the strategic implications of recent intelligence successes and failures, the impact of emerging technologies like artificial intelligence and quantum computing, and the delicate balance between national security and democratic values. This analysis aims to equip decision-makers with a comprehensive understanding of the evolving intelligence landscape, enabling them to make informed choices about resource allocation, risk management, and long-term strategic planning in an era where information is both a powerful weapon and a critical defense.

Key Findings

- Bipartisan cooperation in intelligence oversight is crucial for maintaining the credibility and effectiveness of US intelligence agencies, as demonstrated by the current leadership of the House Permanent Select Committee on Intelligence.

- Recent intelligence failures, such as those related to the Hamas attack on Israel, highlight the need for a renewed focus on human intelligence (HUMINT) capabilities alongside technological solutions.

- The US intelligence community's performance in the Russia-Ukraine conflict, particularly in strategic information sharing, represents a significant shift in approach that has yielded positive results.

- China poses a unique challenge for intelligence gathering due to its technological capabilities and different privacy standards, necessitating a careful balance of traditional and innovative collection methods.

- Emerging technologies, especially artificial intelligence and quantum computing, present both opportunities and risks for intelligence agencies, requiring significant reforms in budget cycles and procurement processes.

- The reauthorization of the Foreign Intelligence Surveillance Act (FISA) Section 702 is a critical priority, with ongoing efforts to balance necessary reforms with maintaining essential intelligence collection capabilities.

- Cybersecurity threats, including potential attacks on critical infrastructure and operating systems, remain a top concern for intelligence agencies and policymakers, with a growing recognition of the need for international norms in cyberspace.

Analysis

The Evolution of Intelligence Oversight

Congressional oversight of US intelligence has entered a new phase of bipartisan cooperation, as exemplified by the current leadership of the House Permanent Select Committee on Intelligence. This approach is crucial for restoring trust in the intelligence community and ensuring its effectiveness in addressing national security challenges. The committee's focus on issues such as reforming budget cycles, addressing the culture of sexual assault, and improving the handling of classified documents demonstrates a commitment to both supporting and scrutinizing intelligence activities.

Balancing Technology and Human Intelligence

Recent events, particularly the intelligence failure surrounding the Hamas attack on Israel, have underscored the ongoing importance of human intelligence alongside technological solutions. While signals intelligence (SIGINT) and imagery intelligence (IMINT) provide valuable data, they cannot fully capture the nuances of human behavior and intentions. The intelligence community must balance investing in cutting-edge technologies and maintaining robust HUMINT capabilities.

Case Study: Russia-Ukraine Conflict

The US intelligence community's performance in the Russia-Ukraine conflict represents a significant success story. The strategic sharing of intelligence with Ukraine and the public marked a shift in approach that proved effective in exposing adversary actions and shaping the narrative. This case demonstrates the potential for intelligence to be used not just for internal decision-making but as a public diplomacy and deterrence tool.

The China Challenge

China presents a unique set of challenges for US intelligence. Its technological capabilities and different approaches to privacy make traditional collection methods increasingly difficult. The intelligence community must navigate the complex economic interdependence between the US and China while developing innovative approaches to gather critical information. This may involve advanced technical collection methods and carefully cultivated human sources.

Technological Frontiers: AI and Quantum Computing

Artificial intelligence and quantum computing represent opportunities and risks for the intelligence community. These technologies have the potential to revolutionize data analysis and cryptography, but they also pose significant challenges in terms of procurement, implementation, and potential vulnerabilities. The current budget and procurement processes could be better-suited to the rapid pace of technological advancement, necessitating reforms to allow for more agile and innovative approaches.

FISA Section 702 and the Balance of Security and Privacy

The ongoing debate surrounding the reauthorization of FISA Section 702 highlights the tension between maintaining critical intelligence capabilities and protecting civil liberties. The intelligence community and lawmakers are working to address past abuses while preserving the ability to collect vital foreign intelligence. This process underscores the need for continuous reassessment and reform of intelligence authorities in light of evolving threats and public concerns.

The Cyber Frontier

Cybersecurity remains a critical concern for the intelligence community. The potential for devastating attacks on critical infrastructure and operating systems necessitates a robust defensive and offensive cyber capability. Moreover, the lack of established international norms in cyberspace creates a volatile environment where the rules of engagement often need to be clarified.

Developing these norms while maintaining a technological edge will be crucial for US intelligence in the coming years.

Recommendations

For Policymakers:

- Prioritize the reform of budget cycles and procurement processes to facilitate faster adoption of emerging technologies in the intelligence community.

- Develop comprehensive legislation to establish clear guidelines for the use of artificial intelligence in intelligence gathering and analysis, balancing innovation with ethical considerations.

- Increase funding for HUMINT capabilities and training to complement technological intelligence-gathering methods.

For Regulators:

- Implement more rigorous oversight mechanisms for the use of FISA Section 702 authorities, including enhanced auditing and reporting requirements.

- Develop clear guidelines for the responsible development and use of quantum computing technologies in the intelligence sector.

- Establish a framework for regular review and update of cybersecurity standards for intelligence agencies and their private sector partners.

For Industry Leaders:

- Increase collaboration with intelligence agencies through public-private partnerships, particularly in the areas of AI, quantum computing, and cybersecurity.

- Invest in developing secure, scalable technologies that can meet the unique needs of the intelligence community while maintaining commercial viability.

- Prioritize the development of tools and technologies that can enhance HUMINT capabilities in an increasingly digital world.

For Civil Society Organizations:

- Advocate for greater transparency in intelligence operations while respecting necessary secrecy for national security.

- Engage in public education initiatives to increase understanding of intelligence issues and their impact on civil liberties.

- Collaborate with policymakers and intelligence agencies to develop ethical frameworks for emerging technologies in intelligence gathering and analysis.

Conclusion

The US intelligence community stands at a critical juncture, facing complex challenges that require innovative solutions and careful navigation of ethical and legal boundaries. By embracing bipartisan cooperation, balancing technological advancements with traditional intelligence-gathering methods, and adapting to emerging threats, the intelligence community can maintain its effectiveness in safeguarding national security.

The recommendations in this report guide policymakers, regulators, industry leaders, and civil society organizations to contribute to this evolution. As we move forward, it is important to recognize that the effectiveness of US intelligence stems from a combination of advanced technological capabilities, skilled operatives, and the ability to safeguard national interests while maintaining ethical standards and accountability.

The future of US intelligence will be shaped by our collective ability to innovate, adapt, and collaborate in the face of rapidly evolving global challenges. The time for strategic action is now.

TWENTY EIGHT

Preparing for the virtual AI revolution: EU's flexible principles imperative

Euractiv, Christophe Carugati, 10ᵗʰ October 2023

The rapid advancement of virtual AI assistants is poised to revolutionize how people interact with technology in their daily lives. As these AI companions become increasingly sophisticated and integral to various aspects of society, there is a pressing need for a regulatory framework that balances innovation with risk mitigation. This report examines the European Union's approach to regulating AI, focusing on the importance of flexible principles in guiding the development and deployment of virtual AI assistants.

The emergence of chatbots like ChatGPT have demonstrated the potential of AI to engage in human-like interactions across a wide range of tasks. However, this transformation brings both opportunities and challenges that regulators must address promptly. By adopting a flexible, principle-based approach, the EU aims to foster innovation while safeguarding against potential pitfalls in the rapidly evolving AI landscape.

Key Findings

- Virtual AI assistants are evolving from task-specific tools to versatile companions capable of complex interactions across multiple domains.

- The EU's regulatory approach emphasizes flexible principles over rigid rules to accommodate the fast-paced nature of AI development.

- Open ecosystems and competition among multiple providers are crucial for fostering innovation and protecting user privacy and safety.

- Existing regulations like the Digital Markets Act (DMA) and General Data Protection Regulation (GDPR) provide a foundation for addressing some AI-related concerns.

- There is a need for additional, AI-specific principles to address unique challenges posed by virtual AI assistants.

Analysis

The virtual AI assistant revolution is characterized by the transformation of AI from narrow, task-specific tools to more generalized, conversational interfaces. Companies like Microsoft, OpenAI, Amazon, Meta, and Google are at the forefront of this evolution, developing AI systems that can engage in human-like interactions across a broad spectrum of topics and tasks.

This shift presents significant opportunities for enhancing productivity, creativity, and user experience. Virtual AI assistants could potentially assist in planning trips, responding to emails, and even serving as digital companions. However, the rapid advancement of these technologies also raises concerns about privacy, data misuse, and the potential for addictive behaviors.

The EU's approach to regulating this emerging field emphasizes flexibility and adaptability. Rather than imposing rigid rules that may quickly become obsolete, the focus is on establishing guiding principles that can evolve alongside the technology. This strategy aims to strike a balance between promoting innovation and mitigating risks.

Key principles proposed for regulating virtual AI assistants include:

- **Access Principle:** Ensuring third-party access to AI ecosystems to prevent monopolistic control and foster competition.

- **Safety-First Principle:** Implementing safeguards to limit harmful or addictive functionalities in AI systems.

- **Privacy Protection:** Upholding stringent data protection standards in line with existing regulations like GDPR.

- **Transparency:** Requiring clear disclosure of AI involvement in user interactions and decision-making processes.

- **Fairness and Non-Discrimination:** Ensuring AI systems do not perpetuate or exacerbate biases.

These principles align with broader EU initiatives like the Digital Markets Act (DMA), which aims to ensure open and fair digital markets. However, the unique challenges posed by AI necessitate additional, specialized guidelines.

The development of virtual AI assistants also raises questions about market dynamics and competition. While there is potential for a diverse ecosystem of AI providers, there is also a risk of market concentration if only a few dominant players emerge. The EU's regulatory approach seeks to prevent such concentration by promoting interoperability and fair competition.

From a technical standpoint, the development of foundation models (FMs) underpins much of the progress in virtual AI assistants. These large-scale models, trained on vast amounts of data, serve as the basis for more specialized applications. The EU's regulatory framework must account for the unique challenges posed by FMs, including issues of data governance, model transparency, and the potential for biased or harmful outputs.

Recommendations

- Develop a set of AI-specific principles that complement existing digital regulations, focusing on the unique challenges posed by virtual AI assistants.

- Establish a mechanism for regular review and updating of these principles to keep pace with technological advancements.

- Encourage collaboration between regulators, industry stakeholders, and academic experts to ensure a well-rounded approach to AI governance.

- Promote research into the societal impacts of virtual AI assistants, including potential effects on mental health, work-life balance, and social interactions.

- Invest in public education initiatives to increase AI literacy and ensure users can make informed decisions about their interactions with virtual AI assistants.

Conclusion

The virtual AI assistant revolution presents both exciting opportunities and significant challenges for society. The EU's approach of adopting flexible principles represents a promising strategy for navigating this complex landscape. By fostering innovation while maintaining safeguards against potential risks, this framework aims to create an environment where AI can flourish responsibly.

As virtual AI assistants become more integrated into daily life, it is crucial that regulatory efforts keep pace with technological advancements. The EU's emphasis on adaptable principles provides a foundation for ongoing dialogue and adjustment as the field evolves. By striking the right balance between innovation and protection, the EU can help shape a future where virtual AI assistants enhance human capabilities while respecting fundamental rights and values.

Further Reading

Bommasani, R., et al. (2021). On the Opportunities and Risks of Foundation Models. arXiv preprint.

European Commission. (2021). Proposal for a Regulation on a European Approach for Artificial Intelligence.

Floridi, L., & Cowls, J. (2019). A Unified Framework of Five Principles for AI in Society. Harvard Data Science Review.

Marcus, G., & Davis, E. (2020). Rebooting AI: Building Artificial Intelligence We Can Trust. Pantheon.

Zuboff, S. (2019). The Age of Surveillance Capitalism: The Fight for a Human Future at the New Frontier of Power. PublicAffairs.

TWENTY NINE

Generative AI poses challenges for Europe

Carnegie Europe, Raluca Csernatoni, 19th October 2023

Generative artificial intelligence (AI) is rapidly evolving, presenting both significant opportunities and challenges for the European Union (EU). This report analyzes the current landscape of generative AI, its potential impact on various sectors, and the EU's response to this technological revolution. Key findings highlight the need for balanced regulation, international cooperation, and strategic investments to harness the benefits of generative AI while mitigating associated risks. The report concludes with actionable recommendations for EU policymakers and senior management to navigate this complex terrain effectively.

Key Takeaways:

- Generative AI models could contribute trillions of dollars to the global economy, but also pose significant risks if not properly regulated.

- The EU is positioning itself as a leader in AI regulation with initiatives like the AI Act and international collaborations.

- Balancing innovation with risk mitigation is crucial for the EU to maintain competitiveness while upholding democratic values.

- Cybersecurity and national security implications of generative AI require urgent attention and strategic planning.

The advent of large generative AI models (LGAIMs) such as ChatGPT, DALL-E, and Midjourney marks a pivotal moment in technological advancement. These models, capable of producing high-quality text, images, audio, and video content, are poised to disrupt numerous industries and reshape the landscape of knowledge production. As the European Union grapples with the implications of this technology, it faces the challenge of fostering innovation while addressing potential risks and ethical concerns.

Key Findings

- Generative AI models have the potential to contribute significantly to the global economy. According to McKinsey, these technologies could add trillions of dollars in value across various sectors. However, this economic potential is accompanied by the risk of widespread disruption to existing business models and labor markets.

- The rapid evolution of generative AI presents a moving target for regulators. The EU's flagship AI

Act, currently under negotiation, aims to provide a risk-based framework for AI regulation. However, there are concerns about whether it can remain future-proof in the face of rapidly advancing technology.

- The EU recognizes the need for international cooperation in AI governance. Initiatives such as the EU-US Trade and Technology Council and the EU-Japan Digital Partnership demonstrate efforts to align approaches with key partners. The G7's International Guiding Principles for organizations developing advanced AI systems is another step towards global norms.

- Generative AI has significant implications for cybersecurity and national security. While it can enhance defensive capabilities, it also enables sophisticated attacks and can be weaponized in ways that threaten elections and military operations.

Analysis

The EU's approach to generative AI is characterized by a desire to lead in regulation while fostering innovation. The emphasis on "trustworthy AI" aligns with European values but must be balanced against the need for competitiveness in a global market.

The call for regulation from tech industry leaders presents a paradox. While they warn of existential risks, their business practices often prioritize rapid deployment over caution. This disconnect highlights the need for robust, independent regulatory frameworks.

The EU's focus on international cooperation is crucial. As the global governance landscape for AI becomes increasingly complex and competitive, the EU's ability to shape norms and standards will depend on effective partnerships and diplomatic efforts.

The security implications of generative AI are particularly concerning. The potential for AI to be used in sophisticated cyber attacks, disinformation campaigns, and military applications necessitates a comprehensive security strategy that incorporates AI considerations.

Recommendations

- **Adaptive Regulation:** Develop a flexible regulatory framework that can evolve with technological advancements. Regularly review and update the AI Act to ensure it remains relevant and effective.

- **Strategic Investments:** Allocate resources to support European AI research and development, focusing on areas where the EU can develop competitive advantages while adhering to ethical principles.

- **International Collaboration:** Strengthen partnerships with like-minded countries to develop common standards and norms for AI governance. Prioritize engagement in multilateral forums to shape global AI policy.

- **AI Security Strategy:** Develop a comprehensive strategy addressing the cybersecurity and national security implications of generative AI. This should include both defensive measures and guidelines for ethical AI use in defense applications.

- **Public-Private Partnerships:** Foster collaboration between government, industry, and academia to ensure that AI development aligns with European values and societal needs.

Conclusion

The generative AI revolution presents Europe with both unprecedented opportunities and significant challenges. By taking a proactive, balanced approach that combines adaptive regulation, strategic investments, and international cooperation, the EU can position itself as a global leader in responsible AI development and use. The recommendations provided offer a roadmap for navigating this complex landscape, ensuring that Europe harnesses the benefits of generative AI while mitigating its risks.

Further Reading

European Commission. (2023). "Artificial Intelligence Act." Brussels: European Union.

McKinsey Global Institute. (2023). "The Economic Potential of Generative AI: The Next Productivity Frontier." New York: McKinsey & Company.

Csernatoni, R. (2023). "Generative AI Poses Challenges for Europe." Carnegie Europe.

G7 Digital and Technology Ministers. (2023). "Hiroshima AI Process: International Guiding Principles for Organizations Developing Advanced AI Systems." G7 Information Centre.

Brundage, M. et al. (2023). "Toward Trustworthy AI Development: Mechanisms for Supporting Verifiable Claims." arXiv preprint arXiv:2004.07213.

THIRTY

Why AI will change the core of foreign policymaking

Global Policy, Cornelius Adebahr, 11th October 2023

Generative artificial intelligence (AI) is rapidly evolving, presenting both significant opportunities and challenges for the European Union (EU). This report analyzes the current landscape of generative AI, its potential impact on various sectors, and the EU's response to this technological revolution. Key findings highlight the need for balanced regulation, international cooperation, and strategic investments to harness the benefits of generative AI while mitigating associated risks. The report concludes with actionable recommendations for EU policymakers and senior management to navigate this complex terrain effectively.

Key Takeaways:

- Generative AI models could contribute trillions of dollars to the global economy but pose significant risks if they are not properly regulated.

- The EU is positioning itself as a leader in AI regulation with initiatives like the AI Act and international collaborations.

- Balancing innovation with risk mitigation is crucial for the EU to maintain competitiveness while upholding democratic values.

- Cybersecurity and national security implications of generative AI require urgent attention and strategic planning.

The advent of large generative AI models (LGAIMs) such as ChatGPT, DALL-E, and Midjourney marks a pivotal moment in technological advancement. These models, capable of producing high-quality text, images, audio, and video content, are poised to disrupt numerous industries and reshape the landscape of knowledge production. As the European Union grapples with the implications of this technology, it faces the challenge of fostering innovation while addressing potential risks and ethical concerns.

Key Findings

- **Economic Potential and Disruption:** Generative AI models have the potential to contribute significantly to the global economy. According to McKinsey, these technologies could add trillions of dollars in value across various sectors. However, this economic potential is accompanied by the risk of widespread disruption to existing business models and labor markets.

- **Regulatory Challenges:** The rapid evolution of generative AI presents a moving target for regulators. The EU's flagship AI Act aims to provide a risk-based framework for AI regulation. However, there are concerns about whether it can remain future-proof in the face of rapidly advancing technology.

- **Global Governance and Cooperation:** The EU recognizes the need for international cooperation in AI governance. Initiatives such as the EU-US Trade and Technology Council and the EU-Japan Digital Partnership demonstrate efforts to align approaches with key partners. The G7's International Guiding Principles for organizations developing advanced AI systems is another step towards global norms.

- **Security Implications:** Generative AI has significant implications for cybersecurity and national security. While it can enhance defensive capabilities, it also enables sophisticated attacks and can be weaponized in ways that threaten elections and military operations.

Analysis

The EU's approach to generative AI is characterized by a desire to lead in regulation while fostering innovation. The emphasis on "trustworthy AI" aligns with European values but must be balanced against the need for competitiveness in a global market.

The call for regulation from tech industry leaders presents a paradox. While they warn of existential risks, their business practices often prioritize rapid deployment over caution. This disconnect highlights the need for robust, independent regulatory frameworks.

The EU's focus on international cooperation is crucial. As the global governance landscape for AI becomes increasingly complex and competitive, the EU's ability to shape norms and standards will depend on effective partnerships and diplomatic efforts.

The security implications of generative AI are particularly concerning. The potential for AI to be used in sophisticated cyber attacks, disinformation campaigns, and military applications necessitates a comprehensive security strategy that incorporates AI considerations.

Recommendations

- **Adaptive Regulation:** Develop a flexible regulatory framework that can evolve with technological advancements. Regularly review and update the AI Act to ensure it remains relevant and effective.

- **Strategic Investments:** Allocate resources to support European AI research and development, focusing on areas where the EU can develop competitive advantages while adhering to ethical principles.

- **International Collaboration:** Strengthen partnerships with like-minded countries to develop common standards and norms for AI governance. Prioritize engagement in multilateral forums to shape global AI policy.

- **AI Security Strategy:** Develop a comprehensive strategy addressing the cybersecurity and national security implications of generative AI. This should include both defensive measures and guidelines for ethical AI use in defense applications.

- **Public-Private Partnerships:** Foster collaboration between government, industry, and academia to ensure that AI development aligns with European values and societal needs.

Conclusion

The generative AI revolution presents Europe with both unprecedented opportunities and significant challenges. By taking a proactive, balanced approach that combines adaptive regulation, strategic investments, and international cooperation, the EU can position itself as a global leader in responsible AI development and use. The recommendations provided offer a roadmap for navigating this complex landscape, ensuring that Europe harnesses the benefits of generative AI while mitigating its risks.

Further Reading

European Commission. (2023). "Artificial Intelligence Act." Brussels: European Union.

McKinsey Global Institute. (2023). "The Economic Potential of Generative AI: The Next Productivity Frontier." New York: McKinsey & Company.

Csernatoni, R. (2023). "Generative AI Poses Challenges for Europe." Carnegie Europe.

G7 Digital and Technology Ministers. (2023). "Hiroshima AI Process: International Guiding Principles for Organizations Developing Advanced AI Systems." G7 Information Centre.

Brundage, M. et al. (2023). "Toward Trustworthy AI Development: Mechanisms for Supporting Verifiable Claims." arXiv preprint arXiv:2004.07213.

THIRTY ONE

Global AI governance is currently like the Tokyo Shibuya crossing - scrambled

Centre for European Policy Studies, Andrea Renda, 05th October 2023

The rapid advancement of generative AI technologies has sparked an urgent global debate on AI governance. This report analyzes the current landscape of AI governance efforts, focusing on the challenges and opportunities for the European Union. Key findings highlight the need for balanced, enforceable regulation, international cooperation, and strategic investments. The report concludes with actionable recommendations for EU policymakers to navigate this complex terrain effectively.

Key Takeaways:

- Global AI governance efforts are fragmented and lack alignment on key issues.

- The EU's AI Act faces delays and challenges amidst the evolving global debate.

- There's a risk of overemphasis on AGI at the expense of "AI for good" applications.

- International cooperation is crucial, but proposed new institutions may be ineffective.

- The EU has an opportunity to lead in responsible AI development and governance.

The emergence of powerful generative AI systems like ChatGPT and Google BARD has intensified the global debate on AI governance. While there's broad agreement on the urgency of the issue, there's little consensus on what actions should be taken, how to implement them, and who should be responsible. This lack of alignment poses significant challenges for policymakers, particularly in the European Union, as they attempt to regulate this rapidly evolving technology.

Key Findings

- **Fragmented Global Governance Landscape:** Various proposals for new institutional architectures have emerged, including an IPCC-like expert panel, an International AI Organization (IAIO), and a Global AI Observatory (GAIO). However, these proposals are unlikely to introduce enforceable guardrails on AI development in the near term.

- **EU Regulatory Challenges:** The EU's AI Act, initially expected in early 2023, has faced delays and challenges. The final text was voted on by the European Parliament in June, but trilogue negotiations are experiencing significant difficulties. The Act is now unlikely to enter into force before 2026.

- **Conflicting Industry Signals:** Tech leaders have sent mixed messages, calling for both regulation and moratoriums while also resisting the classification of generative AI as high-risk. This has complicated the regulatory landscape and potentially weakened ongoing governance efforts.

- **Investment Trends:** There's a risk that emphasis on potential dangers from superhuman intelligence is driving massive investment in AGI start-ups, potentially at the expense of more immediately beneficial "AI for good" applications in areas like climate change, biodiversity, and healthcare.

- **International Initiatives:** The UN Secretary-General has announced the creation of a Multistakeholder Advisory Body focused on making AI available to all and leveraging it for the Sustainable Development Goals. This could provide a more balanced approach to global AI governance.

Analysis

The EU's approach to AI governance is at a critical juncture. While the EU aims to lead in regulation with the AI Act, delays and challenges in its implementation risk leaving a regulatory vacuum. The global debate's focus on long-term existential risks and new institutional architectures may be distracting from more immediate governance needs.

The conflicting signals from industry leaders highlight the complexity of the issue. On one hand, they warn of existential risks; on the other, they resist stringent regulation. This paradox underscores the need for balanced, evidence-based policymaking that can adapt to rapid technological changes.

The risk of overemphasis on AGI development at the expense of "AI for good" applications is particularly concerning. The EU has an opportunity to lead in promoting and incentivizing AI solutions for pressing global challenges like climate change and healthcare.

Recommendations

- **Accelerate and Refine the AI Act:** Prioritize the finalization and implementation of the EU AI Act, ensuring it remains relevant and adaptable to emerging technologies.

- **Promote "AI for Good":** Develop incentives and funding mechanisms to encourage AI applications that address pressing global challenges aligned with the UN Sustainable Development Goals.

- **Engage in Targeted International Cooperation:** Rather than creating new institutions, work within existing frameworks (e.g., OECD, UNESCO) to develop common standards and norms for AI governance.

- **Develop an EU AI Security Strategy:** Create a comprehensive approach addressing both the potential benefits and risks of AI in cybersecurity and national security contexts.

- **Foster Public-Private Collaboration:** Establish structured dialogues between policymakers, industry leaders, and civil society to ensure balanced and effective governance approaches.

Conclusion

The global AI governance landscape remains fragmented and challenging, but it also presents opportunities for the EU to lead in responsible AI development and regulation. By focusing on practical, enforceable measures and promoting "AI for good" applications, the EU can help steer the global debate towards more constructive outcomes. The recommendations provided offer a roadmap for navigating this complex landscape, ensuring that Europe harnesses the benefits of AI while effectively mitigating its risks.

Further Reading

European Commission. (2023). "Artificial Intelligence Act." Brussels: European Union.

Renda, A. (2023). "Global AI governance is currently like the Tokyo Shibuya crossing–scrambled." Centre for European Policy Studies.

United Nations. (2023). "UN Secretary-General's Announcement on the Multistakeholder Advisory Body on AI." New York: United Nations.

OECD. (2023). "OECD AI Principles." Paris: Organization for Economic Co-operation and Development.

UNESCO. (2023). "Recommendation on the Ethics of Artificial Intelligence." Paris: United Nations Educational, Scientific and Cultural Organization.

THIRTY TWO

When we can no longer believe our eyes and ears

German Institute for International and Security Affairs, Aldo Kleeman, 26th October 2023

Deepfakes (artificially created or altered media content that appears authentic) are rapidly emerging as a significant threat to information integrity, particularly in conflict situations. As the technology improves, deepfakes are becoming increasingly difficult to detect, raising concerns about their potential for abuse in disinformation campaigns. This report examines the current state of deepfake technology, its potential applications in conflicts, and strategies for mitigating associated risks.

Key Takeaways:

- Deepfake quality is improving rapidly due to AI advancements, increased computing power, and access to large training datasets.

- Potential malicious uses in conflicts include dividing allies, mobilizing populations, and creating fear and uncertainty.

- Both preventive measures (e.g., access restrictions, labeling) and reactive approaches (e.g., detection methods, rapid response) are necessary to combat deepfakes.

The proliferation of deepfake technology represents a paradigm shift in the landscape of media manipulation and disinformation. While propaganda and misinformation have long been tools of warfare, the ease with which highly convincing fake media can now be created using AI-powered tools has introduced new dimensions of complexity to the information battlespace. This report analyzes the implications of deepfake technology for conflicts and information warfare, and outlines strategies for addressing this emerging threat.

Key Findings

- **Rapid technological advancement:** Deepfake quality is improving at an accelerating rate, driven by developments in AI, increased computing power, and access to vast training datasets. This is making deepfakes increasingly difficult to distinguish from authentic media.

- **Generative Adversarial Networks (GANs):** Deepfakes are primarily created using GANs, which pit two neural networks against each other - a generator that creates fake media and a discriminator that evaluates authenticity. This process results in increasingly convincing fabrications.

- **Widespread examples:** High-profile deepfake examples now include fabricated videos of political leaders like Barack Obama and Angela Merkel, as well as manipulated images of public figures in controversial situations shared on social media.

- **Evolving disinformation landscape:** The use of generative AI to produce deepfakes has fundamentally altered the nature of disinformation campaigns by increasing the quantity, quality, and ease of production of fabricated media content.

- **Conflict applications:** Deepfakes could be used in conflicts to paralyze or divide allies, mobilize populations against security forces, or create fear and uncertainty among armed forces and the public.

Analysis

The rise of deepfake technology presents a complex challenge for governments, militaries, and security organizations. The ability to create highly convincing fake media content at scale introduces new vectors for disinformation and psychological warfare. In conflict situations, deepfakes could be leveraged to:

- Sow discord among allies by fabricating evidence of betrayal or controversial statements

- Mobilize populations against security forces through manufactured incidents

- Demoralize armed forces with fake videos of leaders surrendering or questioning the mission

- Undermine public support by fabricating atrocities allegedly committed by friendly forces

The potential for deepfakes to rapidly spread misinformation and influence public opinion makes them a powerful tool for information warfare. As deepfake technology becomes more accessible, both state and non-state actors may increasingly incorporate it into their disinformation arsenals.

Countering the deepfake threat requires a multi-faceted approach combining both preventive and reactive measures:

Preventive measures

- Restricting access to deepfake creation tools and training data

- Implementing mandatory labeling for synthetic media

- Raising public awareness about deepfakes and media literacy

- Promoting the creation and dissemination of verifiably authentic content

Reactive approaches

- Developing advanced technical detection methods for identifying deepfakes

- Establishing rapid response protocols to quickly debunk and counter fake content

- Fostering international cooperation on deepfake detection and mitigation strategies

While complete prevention of deepfakes is likely impossible, a robust combination of technological, policy, and education-based approaches can help limit their impact and preserve information integrity.

Recommendations

- **Invest in deepfake detection capabilities:** Allocate resources to develop and acquire cutting-edge technical solutions for identifying synthetic media. This may include AI-powered detection tools and forensic analysis capabilities.

- **Establish a rapid response team:** Create a dedicated unit capable of quickly identifying, analyzing, and countering deepfake content. This team should have cross-functional expertise in technical analysis, strategic communications, and media operations.

- **Develop a comprehensive media literacy program:** Implement training initiatives to educate personnel and the public about deepfakes, their potential impacts, and how to critically evaluate media authenticity.

- **Foster international partnerships:** Collaborate with allies and partners to share best practices, intelligence, and technical capabilities related to deepfake detection and mitigation.

- **Review and update information warfare doctrine:** Reassess existing policies and strategies in light of the deepfake threat, incorporating new defensive and offensive considerations as appropriate.

Conclusion

Deepfake technology represents a significant evolution in the realm of information warfare and disinformation. As the quality and accessibility of deepfakes continue to improve, their potential for abuse in conflict situations grows correspondingly. Addressing this threat will require a coordinated effort across government, military, and civilian sectors, combining technological innovation, policy adaptation, and public education. By proactively developing robust detection and response capabilities, organizations can better position themselves to maintain information integrity in an increasingly complex digital landscape.

Further Reading

Chesney, R., & Citron, D. (2019). Deep Fakes: A Looming Challenge for Privacy, Democracy, and National Security. California Law Review.

Westerlund, M. (2019). The Emergence of Deepfake Technology: A Review. Technology Innovation Management Review.

Kietzmann, J., et al. (2020). Deepfakes: Trick or treat? Business Horizons.

Caldwell, M., et al. (2020). AI-enabled future crime. Crime Science.

Greengard, S. (2020). Will deepfakes do deep damage? Communications of the ACM.

THIRTY THREE

A global declaration on free and open AI

Center for Data Innovation, Daniel Castro, 13th September 2023

A coalition of international organizations has proposed a global declaration on "free and open AI" to ensure generative artificial intelligence (AI) technologies serve democratic ideals and promote global progress. This declaration aims to establish principles for the responsible development and use of AI, particularly large language models (LLMs), as they become integral to society and the economy. The proposal emphasizes protecting freedom of expression, innovation, and trade while promoting transparency and responsible use of AI. This report analyzes the significance of the proposed declaration and provides recommendations for senior leaders.

Key Takeaways:

- Generative AI and LLMs are poised to significantly impact free expression and economic opportunities globally

- The declaration aims to counter potential authoritarian efforts to control or suppress AI-facilitated speech

- Key principles include promoting freedom of expression, protecting innovation and trade, encouraging responsible use, and embracing transparency

- International collaboration is emphasized to develop standards and agreements promoting free and open AI

As generative AI emerges as a transformative technology, democratic nations seek to establish guiding principles to ensure these powerful tools align with democratic values. This proposed declaration builds on previous efforts to promote a "free and open Internet" and aims to provide a framework for the responsible development and deployment of AI technologies, particularly large language models (LLMs).

Key Findings

- **Generative AI as a pivotal technology:** LLMs and other generative AI tools are positioned to become integral to communication, information access, and economic activity across all levels of society.

- **Potential for authoritarian control:** There are concerns that authoritarian regimes may attempt to restrict or manipulate AI models to suppress free expression, as seen in China's efforts to limit AI outputs that challenge regime authority.

- **Emphasis on freedom and openness:** The declaration promotes freedom to create and use AI for legitimate purposes without undue government restrictions, while also emphasizing transparency in AI development and deployment.

- **Balancing risks and benefits:** While acknowledging risks like misinformation, the proposal argues that fostering responsible use and more speech is preferable to censorship or excessive restrictions.

- **International cooperation:** The declaration calls for collaboration between governments and the private sector to develop standards and trade agreements that promote global access to AI tools.

Analysis

The proposed declaration represents a proactive attempt to establish norms and principles for AI governance before the technology becomes fully entrenched in global systems. By emphasizing freedom of expression, innovation, and transparency, the declaration aims to create a framework that aligns AI development with democratic values.

The principles outlined in the declaration seek to strike a balance between fostering innovation and addressing potential risks. Rather than advocating for strict regulations or restrictions, the proposal emphasizes education, responsible use, and counter-speech mechanisms to address concerns like misinformation or hate speech.

The call for international cooperation and standardization is particularly noteworthy, as it recognizes the global nature of AI development and deployment. Establishing common principles across democratic nations could help create a united front against potential authoritarian misuse of AI technologies.

However, the declaration's effectiveness will depend on widespread adoption and enforcement mechanisms, which are not fully detailed in the current proposal. Additionally, tensions may arise between the ideals of openness and the commercial interests of AI developers who may wish to protect proprietary technologies.

Recommendations

- **Engage in international dialogues:** Participate in discussions around the proposed declaration and similar initiatives to help shape global AI governance frameworks.

- **Assess internal AI policies:** Review existing organizational policies related to AI development and use to ensure alignment with principles of freedom, openness, and transparency.

- **Invest in AI literacy:** Develop programs to educate employees and stakeholders about responsible AI use and the principles outlined in the declaration.

- **Foster public-private partnerships:** Collaborate with government agencies and other organizations to develop standards and best practices for free and open AI.

- **Monitor global AI regulations:** Stay informed about emerging AI regulations and governance frameworks in different countries to ensure compliance and identify potential impacts on operations.

Conclusion

The proposed global declaration on free and open AI represents an important step towards establishing democratic principles in the rapidly evolving field of generative AI. While challenges remain in implementation and enforcement, the declaration provides a valuable framework for discussions on AI governance. Organizations should closely monitor developments in this area and proactively engage in shaping policies that promote responsible AI development and use.

Further Reading

Artificial Intelligence Act (European Union)

OECD AI Principles

UNESCO Recommendation on the Ethics of Artificial Intelligence

National AI strategies (various countries)

"The Age of AI: And Our Human Future" by Henry Kissinger, Eric Schmidt, and Daniel Huttenlocher

THIRTY FOUR

How Europe can make the most of AI

Centre for European Reform, Zach Myers and John Springford, 14th October 2023

As artificial intelligence (AI) emerges as a transformative technology with significant potential to boost productivity and economic growth, the European Union (EU) must strategically position itself to capitalize on the opportunities while mitigating risks. This report analyzes the key challenges and opportunities for Europe in the AI landscape and provides recommendations for policymakers and business leaders to maximize the benefits of AI adoption.

Key Takeaways:

- AI, particularly large language models (LLMs), can potentially boost Europe's slow-growing economy by raising productivity in services industries

- The EU should focus on encouraging European businesses to adopt and exploit AI technology rather than replicating foreign innovations

- Ensuring competition between AI foundation models is crucial for European businesses to access a range of choices at fair prices

- Supporting AI adoption through research grants, tax incentives, and digital skills development is essential

- The proposed AI Act provides a basis for addressing higher-risk AI uses but requires refinement to avoid hindering low-risk AI adoption

As AI technologies rapidly evolve, the European Union faces the challenge of harnessing their potential to drive economic growth while maintaining alignment with European values and regulatory frameworks. This report examines strategies for Europe to maximize the benefits of AI adoption across its economy.

Key Findings

- **Economic potential:** AI, especially large language models, has the potential to significantly boost productivity growth in Europe's service industries, which have historically underinvested in technology compared to American counterparts.

- **Focus on adoption:** Rather than attempting to replicate foreign AI innovations, the EU should prioritize ensuring European businesses effectively adopt and exploit existing AI technologies.

- **Competition in AI models:** Maintaining a competitive market for AI foundation models is crucial to ensure European businesses have access to a range of choices at fair prices.

- **Barriers to adoption:** Key challenges include the need for digital skills development, regulatory uncertainties, and potential underinvestment in AI research and deployment.

- **Regulatory balance:** The proposed AI Act provides a framework for addressing high-risk AI uses but requires refinement to avoid inadvertently hindering low-risk AI adoption.

Analysis

Europe's approach to AI must balance the imperative for rapid adoption with the need to align AI development and deployment with European values and regulatory standards. The focus on adoption rather than replication of foreign innovations represents a pragmatic strategy, given the current global AI landscape.

The emphasis on ensuring competition between AI foundation models is particularly noteworthy. While barriers to entry in the AI market exist, the current market appears diverse and dynamic. Maintaining this competitive environment will be crucial for European businesses to access a range of AI solutions at fair prices.

The proposed support mechanisms, including research grants, tax incentives, and investments in digital skills development, address critical barriers to AI adoption. However, the effectiveness of these measures will depend on their implementation and the ability to create a supportive ecosystem for AI innovation and deployment.

The proposed AI Act represents a significant step towards creating a consistent EU-wide approach to AI governance. However, the report rightly identifies the need for refinements to strike the right balance between risk mitigation and innovation encouragement. Clarifying definitions, delineating responsibilities across the AI value chain, and avoiding inadvertent regulation of existing low-risk technologies will be crucial in this regard.

Recommendations

- **Prioritize AI adoption:** Policymakers should focus on incentivizing and supporting European businesses, particularly in the services sector, to adopt and integrate AI technologies into their operations.

- **Foster competition:** Maintain a regulatory environment that encourages competition between AI foundation models to ensure a diverse and innovative AI ecosystem.

- **Invest in skills:** Develop comprehensive programs to enhance digital and AI-related skills across the European workforce, focusing on both technical and applied AI skills.

- **Refine the AI Act:** Work to clarify and refine the proposed AI Act to ensure it effectively addresses high-risk AI uses without unduly burdening low-risk applications.

- **Support research and deployment:** Implement targeted grant programs and tax incentives to encourage AI research and deployment, particularly among small and medium-sized enterprises.

Conclusion

Europe stands at a critical juncture in the global AI landscape. By focusing on widespread adoption of AI technologies, fostering a competitive AI market, and refining its regulatory approach, the EU can position itself to leverage AI's transformative potential. The most significant risk for Europe lies not in the deployment of AI but in failing to adopt it swiftly and effectively. With strategic action and policy refinement, Europe can harness AI to drive productivity growth, maintain international competitiveness, and shape the future of AI in alignment with its values.

Further Reading

European Commission, "Proposal for a Regulation on Artificial Intelligence" (AI Act)

OECD, "AI Adoption in the Enterprise: Trends and Challenges"

McKinsey Global Institute, "Notes from the AI Frontier: Tackling Europe's Gap in Digital and AI"

World Economic Forum, "Artificial Intelligence and Robotics"

European Parliament Research Service, "The impact of the General Data Protection Regulation (GDPR) on artificial intelligence"

THIRTY FIVE

From risk to revolution: How AI can revive democracy

Chatham House, Alex Krasodomski, 29th September 2023

As artificial intelligence (AI) continues to advance rapidly, there is growing recognition of its potential to pose risks, revolutionize public institutions, and reinvigorate democratic processes. This report analyzes the opportunities for governments to leverage AI to enhance public services, increase citizen engagement, and address complex global challenges. It provides recommendations for policymakers and leaders to harness AI's transformative potential in the public sector.

Key Takeaways:

- AI offers opportunities to reverse decades of underinvestment in public sector capacity and revitalize democratic processes

- Governments must move beyond regulation to actively design, develop and deploy AI systems serving the public good

- International collaboration on public AI development can make systems more robust and effective

- AI-powered tools for citizen engagement and collective decision-making show promise for enhancing democracy

- Building sovereign AI capabilities is crucial for governments to avoid overreliance on private tech companies

As governments and industries convene to discuss AI safety and regulation, an alternative approach is emerging that emphasizes the proactive development of public AI systems. This report examines how governments can leverage AI to transform public institutions, enhance democratic engagement, and address pressing societal challenges.

Key Findings

- **Public sector potential:** AI offers significant opportunities to reverse the trend of underinvestment in public institutions and reinvigorate democratic processes.

- **Shifting government role:** To realize AI's public benefits, governments must move beyond regulation to actively participate in AI design, development, and deployment.

- **International collaboration:** Cooperation between nations on public AI development can produce more robust and effective systems while also addressing global governance challenges.

- **Democratic innovation:** AI-powered tools for citizen engagement and collective decision-making show early promise for enhancing democratic participation.

- **Sovereign capabilities:** Building in-house AI expertise and resources is crucial for governments to avoid overreliance on private tech companies.

Analysis

The prevailing narrative around AI governance has focused heavily on the need for government regulation to mitigate potential risks. However, this approach fails to capitalize on the transformative potential of AI to enhance public institutions and democratic processes. By taking a more active role in AI development, governments can shape the technology to serve the public good rather than solely private interests.

Several key factors make this shift in approach both necessary and timely:

- **Technological power imbalance:** The outsized influence of technology companies in political and geopolitical spheres highlights the need for governments to develop sovereign AI capabilities. Without this, critical decisions affecting citizens may be left to unaccountable private actors.

- **Democratic innovation opportunities:** Early experiments with AI-powered tools for citizen engagement and collective decision-making, such as vTaiwan, demonstrate the potential to significantly enhance democratic participation and responsiveness.

- **International collaboration potential:** Pooling public AI resources and expertise across nations could produce more robust systems while also addressing global governance challenges that transcend borders.

- **Public sector modernization:** AI offers a path to reverse decades of underinvestment in public sector capacity and bring government services and processes into the 21st century.

- **Market creation for beneficial AI:** Government procurement requirements for transparency, accuracy, and fairness in AI systems can help drive the development of more trustworthy and socially beneficial AI tools.

However, realizing these benefits will require overcoming several challenges, including:

- Resource and expertise gaps between public and private sectors in AI development

- The need to ensure democratic accountability and transparency in public AI systems

- Balancing international collaboration with national interests and security concerns

- Resistance to changing established democratic and bureaucratic processes

---

Recommendations

- **Invest in sovereign AI capabilities:** Allocate significant resources to building in-house AI expertise, computing infrastructure, and development capacity within government.

- **Foster public-private partnerships:** Collaborate with industry and academia to accelerate public AI development while maintaining democratic oversight.

- **Pursue international collaboration:** Work with allied nations to pool AI resources, share best practices, and develop common standards for public AI systems.

- **Experiment with AI-enhanced democracy:** Pilot AI-powered tools for citizen engagement, participatory decision-making, and policy development.

- **Create markets for beneficial AI:** Use government procurement requirements to incentivize the development of transparent, fair, and trustworthy AI systems.

- **Modernize governance structures:** Update legislative and administrative processes to better incorporate AI-driven insights and citizen input.

- **Prioritize AI education:** Invest in programs to build AI literacy among public servants, elected officials, and the general public.

Conclusion

AI presents a transformative opportunity to revitalize public institutions and democratic processes, but realizing this potential requires a shift in how governments approach the technology. By moving beyond regulation to active development and deployment of public AI systems, governments can shape the future of AI to better serve societal needs. While challenges remain, proactive investment in sovereign AI capabilities and international collaboration can position democracies to thrive in the age of AI.

Further Reading

Mazzucato, M. (2021). Mission Economy: A Moonshot Guide to Changing Capitalism

Noveck, B. S. (2015). Smart Citizens, Smarter State: The Technologies of Expertise and the Future of Governing

O'Reilly, T. (2021). Government as a Platform, Seriously: How a New Tech Stack and Mindset Can Make Government Better

Mulgan, G. (2019). Social Innovation: How Societies Find the Power to Change

Susskind, J. (2018). Future Politics: Living Together in a World Transformed by Tech

THIRTY SIX

Why AI must be decolonized to fulfil its true potential

Chatham House, Dr Mahlet Zimeta, 29th September 2023

As artificial intelligence (AI) rapidly advances, primarily driven by the American private sector, there are growing concerns about its potential to perpetuate and amplify colonial harms. This report analyzes the need to decolonize AI to ensure its development and deployment benefit all of humanity, rather than exacerbating existing inequalities. It provides recommendations for policymakers, business leaders, and AI researchers to foster a more inclusive and equitable approach to AI development.

Key Takeaways:

- AI risks becoming a new vector of colonial harm if not developed with a decolonial mindset

- Data gaps and biases in AI training data limit its potential benefits and could widen existing inequalities

- Extractive business models driving AI development mirror harmful colonial practices

- Decolonizing AI involves fostering diverse perspectives and addressing structural inequalities

- ESG-style reporting for the digital economy is needed to ensure responsible AI development

As AI emerges as a transformative technology with global impact, there is a growing recognition of the need to decolonize its development to prevent the perpetuation of historical injustices and ensure its benefits are equitably distributed. This report examines the colonial risks associated with current AI development practices and explores strategies for fostering a more inclusive and ethical approach to AI.

Key Findings

- **Data bias and gaps:** Significant disparities exist in the data used to train AI models, particularly in areas like genomic research, limiting AI's potential benefits for diverse populations.

- **Public sector challenges:** Colonial erasure of communities has led to underrepresentation in contemporary national statistics, affecting AI development for public services.

- **Extractive business models:** Many AI developments are driven by business practices that mirror harmful colonial extraction methods.

- **Environmental and social impacts:** The environmental costs and exploitative labor practices associated with AI development disproportionately affect marginalized communities.

- **Lack of diverse perspectives:** Current AI development often needs to incorporate diverse epistemologies and ontologies, limiting its potential to address global challenges.

- **Need for more governance:** The lack of ESG-equivalent reporting for the digital economy undermines progress towards sustainable development goals.

Analysis

The rapid advancement of AI, primarily driven by the American private sector, risks recreating colonial power dynamics and exacerbating global inequalities. Several key factors contribute to this risk:

- **Data bias and gaps:** The underrepresentation of diverse populations in AI training data, exemplified by the concentration of genomic research on people of European ancestry, limits AI's potential benefits and could widen existing health disparities.

- **Public sector limitations:** The colonial erasure of communities has led to ongoing underrepresentation in national statistics, affecting the development of AI for public services across various government functions.

- **Extractive business models:** Many AI developments are driven by business practices that mirror colonial extraction methods, prioritizing profit over societal benefit and environmental sustainability.

- **Labor exploitation:** The often traumatizing "ghost work" of data labeling for AI systems is frequently outsourced to low-wage workers in developing countries, perpetuating exploitative labor practices.

- **Environmental impact:** The environmental costs of developing and running AI systems disproportionately affect marginalized global communities, echoing colonial-era resource exploitation.

- **Lack of diverse perspectives:** The dominance of Western perspectives in AI development limits its potential to address global challenges and meet the needs of diverse populations.

- **Need for more governance:** The lack of ESG-equivalent reporting for the digital economy allows colonial legacies to persist in global supply chains and business activities related to AI development.

Addressing these issues requires a concerted effort to decolonize AI, fostering a more inclusive and equitable approach to its development and deployment.

Recommendations

- **Diversify AI training data:** Invest in initiatives to collect and incorporate diverse, globally representative data sets for AI model training.

- **Implement AI equity audits:** Develop and mandate regular audits of AI systems to identify and address biases and potential negative impacts on marginalized communities.

- **Foster inclusive AI development:** Actively incorporate diverse perspectives, including indigenous epistemologies and ontologies, in AI research and development processes.

- **Establish digital economy ESG standards:** Develop and implement ESG-equivalent reporting standards for the AI and digital technology sectors.

- **Promote ethical AI labor practices:** Implement and enforce fair labor standards for all workers involved in AI development, including data labelers and content moderators.

- **Invest in global AI capacity building:** Support initiatives to build AI research and development capabilities in underrepresented regions and communities.

- **Prioritize AI for social good:** Incentivize AI research and development that explicitly addresses societal needs and considers potential negative impacts.

Conclusion

Decolonizing AI is essential to ensure that this powerful technology serves as a force for global progress rather than a means of perpetuating historical injustices. By addressing data biases, fostering diverse perspectives, and implementing responsible development practices, we can harness AI's potential to build a more equitable and sustainable future for all. This requires a collaborative effort from policymakers, industry leaders, researchers, and civil society to reshape the AI landscape with a decolonial mindset.

Further Reading

Birhane, A., et al. (2022). "The Values Encoded in Machine Learning Research"

Gebru, T., et al. (2021). "On the Dangers of Stochastic Parrots: Can Language Models Be Too Big?"

Hao, K. (2022). "Artificial Intelligence is Creating a New Colonial World Order"

Mohamed, S., et al. (2020). "Decolonial AI: Decolonial Theory as Sociotechnical Foresight in Artificial Intelligence"

Benjamin, R. (2019). "Race After Technology: Abolitionist Tools for the New Jim Code"

THIRTY SEVEN

The President's inbox recap: AI's impact on the 2024 US elections

Council on Foreign Relations, Michelle Kurilla, 16th September 2023

As artificial intelligence (AI) continues to advance rapidly, there is growing concern about its potential to significantly impact the integrity of democratic elections. This report analyzes the risks and opportunities presented by AI in the context of the upcoming 2024 US elections. It provides recommendations for policymakers, election officials, and technology leaders to mitigate potential threats while leveraging AI's capabilities to enhance democratic processes.

Key Takeaways:

- AI is expected to exacerbate existing challenges to democracy, particularly around misinformation and trust

- Deepfakes and personalized AI-generated content pose significant risks to voter perception and decision making

- Both major political parties are already leveraging AI in their campaign strategies

- No single solution exists to fully address AI-related election risks; a multi-faceted approach is necessary

- Media literacy and content labeling show promise but also present challenges in implementation

As the 2024 US elections approach, the potential for AI to influence voter behavior and undermine democratic processes has become a critical concern. This report examines the current state of AI use in political campaigns, potential risks to election integrity, and strategies for mitigating these risks while harnessing AI's potential benefits.

Key Findings

- **Democracy under stress:** AI is likely to amplify existing challenges faced by polarized democracies, particularly around the spread of misinformation and erosion of trust in institutions.

- **Deepfake proliferation:** The increasing sophistication of AI-generated deepfakes poses a significant threat to voter perception of reality and candidate integrity.

- **Personalized manipulation:** AI's ability to generate high volumes of unique, personalized content enables more targeted and potentially effective voter manipulation.

- **Broader targets:** AI-powered attacks are not limited to candidates but may also target journalists and other democratic institutions, undermining reliable information sources.

- **Current campaign use:** Both major US political parties are already leveraging AI in their 2024 election strategies, from creating attack ads to drafting fundraising emails.

Analysis

The rapid advancement of AI technologies presents both opportunities and significant risks for democratic elections. Several key factors contribute to the potential for AI to impact the 2024 US elections:

- **Deepfake proliferation:** The increasing quality and accessibility of deepfake technology make it easier to create convincing false videos or audio of candidates, potentially swaying voter opinions or creating confusion about real events.

- **Personalized content generation:** AI's ability to rapidly produce unique, targeted content allows for more sophisticated and potentially effective voter manipulation campaigns.

- **Erosion of truth:** The prevalence of AI-generated content may contribute to a growing "nihilism about the existence of objective truth," making it easier to dismiss any unfavorable information as fake.

- **Institutional targets:** AI-powered disinformation campaigns may target candidates, journalists, and other democratic institutions, undermining trusted sources of information.

- **Dual-use nature:** As demonstrated by current campaign practices, AI can be used for both legitimate and potentially manipulative purposes in political campaigns.

- **Mitigation challenges:** No single solution exists to fully address the risks posed by AI in elections. Proposed strategies like content labeling and media literacy education present their own challenges and limitations.

The complexity and rapidly evolving nature of AI technology make it difficult for policymakers and election officials to develop comprehensive strategies to mitigate risks. However, failure to address these challenges could have significant consequences for the integrity of democratic processes.

Recommendations

- Develop AI-specific election guidelines: Create clear guidelines for the use of AI in political campaigns, including transparency requirements for AI-generated content.

- Invest in detection technology: Allocate resources to develop and deploy advanced AI-generated content detection tools for election officials and media organizations.

- Enhance media literacy programs: Expand and improve media literacy education initiatives to help voters better identify and critically evaluate AI-generated content.

- Implement content labeling standards: Develop and promote standardized labeling practices for AI-generated political content, while being mindful of potential unintended consequences.

- Foster cross-sector collaboration: Encourage partnerships between tech companies, academic institutions, and government agencies to address AI-related election security challenges.

- Strengthen platform policies: Work with social media and content platforms to develop and enforce stricter policies around AI-generated political content and deepfakes.

- Conduct regular risk assessments: Implement ongoing evaluations of AI-related risks to election integrity and adjust mitigation strategies accordingly.

Conclusion

The potential impact of AI on the 2024 US elections presents a complex challenge that requires a multi-faceted and adaptive approach. While AI offers opportunities to enhance certain aspects of the democratic process, its potential for misuse in spreading disinformation and manipulating voter perceptions poses significant risks. By implementing a combination of technological, educational, and policy-based solutions, stakeholders can work to mitigate these risks and preserve the integrity of democratic elections in the age of AI.

Further Reading

Chesney, R. and Citron, D. (2019). "Deep Fakes: A Looming Challenge for Privacy, Democracy, and National Security"

Woolley, S.C. and Howard, P.N. (2018). "Computational Propaganda: Political Parties, Politicians, and Political Manipulation on Social Media"

Persily, N. (2019). "The Internet's Challenge to Democracy: Framing the Problem and Assessing Reforms"

Raska, M. (2021). "Artificial Intelligence and Global Security: Future Trends, Threats and Considerations"

West, D.M. (2018). "The Future of Work: Robots, AI, and Automation"

THIRTY EIGHT

ChatGPT, chatbots, and more: How is Artificial Intelligence being used in corporate HR departments?

IFO Institute, 20th September 2023

Artificial Intelligence (AI) is beginning to revolutionize corporate human resources (HR) departments, offering promising benefits in process automation, recruitment, and various HR functions. However, adoption remains limited due to expertise, legal issues, and trust concerns. This report, based on the Randstad ifo Personnel Manager Survey, provides a comprehensive analysis of the current state of AI adoption in HR, highlighting usage patterns, perceived benefits, and challenges.

Key findings indicate that while only 5% of companies currently use AI in HR, 25% plan to implement it soon. ChatGPT emerges as the most commonly used AI tool, primarily in recruiting and automation. Companies recognize AI's potential in process automation and recruitment, yet face significant barriers, including a need for more expertise and legal concerns.

As AI technologies continue to advance, their potential applications in HR are expanding. This report examines the current state of AI adoption in corporate HR departments, focusing on usage patterns, perceived benefits, and challenges based on recent survey data from German companies. The goal is to provide HR leaders with actionable insights to navigate the evolving landscape of AI in HR.

Key Findings

- **Limited but Growing Adoption:** Only 5% of surveyed companies currently use AI in HR, but 25% plan to implement it in the future.

- **Sector Variations:** Manufacturing shows the highest potential for future AI adoption in HR at 40%, compared to 18% in services and 14% in trade.

- **Tool Preferences:** ChatGPT is the most widely used AI tool (8% of companies) followed by various applications in recruiting automation and chatbots.

- **Preparatory Actions:** 25% of companies are taking actions related to AI use, primarily through working groups and training courses.

- **Significant Concerns:** 86% of companies express concerns about AI adoption, with lack of expertise (62%) and legal aspects (48%) topping the list.

- **Recognized Potential:** Companies see the highest potential for AI in process automation and recruitment/applicant management.

- **Limited Impact on Staffing:** 84% of companies expect their HR staffing levels to remain unchanged due to AI adoption over the next five years.

Analysis

The survey results reveal a cautious approach to AI adoption in HR, with most companies still in the planning or consideration phase. This hesitancy can be attributed to several factors:

- **Expertise Gap:** The lack of in-house AI expertise is the most significant barrier, indicating a need for targeted training and skill development in HR departments. Many companies are forming working groups and conducting training courses to bridge this gap.

- **Legal Uncertainties:** Concerns about the legal aspects of AI use suggest a need for clearer regulatory frameworks and guidance for HR applications. Companies worry about compliance and potential legal repercussions.

- **Trust Deficit:** A third of companies express a lack of trust in AI, highlighting the importance of transparent and explainable AI systems in HR contexts. Building trust through transparency and clear communication about AI's role and limitations is crucial.

- **Implementation Challenges:** Time, effort, and cost considerations also factor into companies' reluctance to adopt AI in HR. The initial investment and integration of AI systems can be daunting, particularly for smaller companies.

Despite these challenges, companies recognize AI's potential to enhance HR processes, particularly in automation and recruitment. This suggests that as barriers are addressed and successful use cases emerge, adoption rates are likely to increase.

Recommendations

- **Develop AI Expertise:** Invest in training programs to build in-house AI skills within HR teams, focusing on practical applications relevant to HR processes.

- **Start Small:** Begin with pilot projects in areas with high perceived potential, such as process automation or recruitment, to gain experience and demonstrate value.

- **Address Legal Concerns:** Work with legal departments and external experts to develop clear guidelines for AI use in HR that comply with relevant regulations.

- **Build Trust:** Implement transparent AI systems and communicate clearly with employees about how AI is being used in HR processes.

- **Explore Partnerships:** Consider collaborating with AI vendors or consultancies to access expertise and accelerate implementation.

- **Monitor Sector Trends:** Stay informed about AI adoption patterns in your industry to identify competitive advantages and best practices.

- **Prepare for the Future:** While immediate staffing impacts may be limited, develop long-term strategies for integrating AI into HR operations and upskilling staff.

Conclusion

AI adoption in corporate HR departments is still in its early stages, with significant growth potential in the coming years. While concerns about expertise, legal issues, and trust present barriers, companies recognize AI's potential to enhance key HR functions. By taking a strategic, measured approach to AI implementation and addressing key concerns, HR leaders can position their organizations to leverage the benefits of AI while mitigating associated risks.

Further Reading

Tambe, P., Cappelli, P., & Yakubovich, V. (2019). Artificial Intelligence in Human Resources Management: Challenges and a Path Forward. California Management Review.

Hmoud, B., & Laszlo, V. (2019). Will Artificial Intelligence Take Over Human Resources Recruitment and Selection? Network Intelligence Studies.

Gartner (2022). Artificial Intelligence Use Cases in Human Resources.

World Economic Forum (2023). The Future of Jobs Report 2023.

MIT Sloan Management Review (2023). The 2023 State of Human Capital Survey: AI in HR.

THIRTY NINE

Employing artificial intelligence and the edge continuum for joint operations

Atlantic Council, General James E. Cartwright and Jags Kandasamy, 18th August 2023

This report analyzes a proposed four-layer edge computing architecture for the US Department of Defense (DOD) to operationalize artificial intelligence (AI) and the edge continuum for Joint All-Domain Command and Control (JADC2). The architecture aims to address challenges in executing the "sense," "make sense," and "act" cycle on vast amounts of data generated by DOD operations in denied, disrupted, intermittent, and limited-bandwidth (DDIL) network environments. By distributing computing power and processing data closer to the source, this approach offers significant advantages in real-time decision-making and operational efficiency.

Key Takeaways:

- **The proposed architecture consists of four layers:** Tactical, Operational, Command, and Strategic Edge.

- AI and machine learning at the edge enable real-time data analysis and decision-making in DDIL environments.

- The architecture aligns with the JADC2 strategy to maintain command-and-control capabilities across domains.

- Distributed computing power allows for executing the "sense," "make sense," and "act" cycle closer to the edge.

- The approach addresses data bottlenecks and enhances decision-making at various operational levels.

As military operations become increasingly data-driven, the US Department of Defense faces challenges in efficiently processing and analyzing vast amounts of information generated by its operations, particularly in remote and hostile environments. This report examines a proposed four-layer edge computing architecture that leverages artificial intelligence and the edge continuum to address these challenges and support the Joint All-Domain Command and Control (JADC2) strategy.

Key Findings

- **Data Bottlenecks and Sensor Proliferation:** The DOD has deployed numerous sensors across various domains, generating massive amounts of data. However, communication networks need to catch up with the expanding data and sensor locations, creating bottlenecks in data transmission and processing.

- **AI and Machine Learning as Optimal Solutions:** Artificial intelligence and machine learning algorithms have emerged as the most effective means of making sense of the growing volume, velocity, and variety of sensor-generated data. The rise of AI at the edge presents a significant opportunity for the DOD to filter signals from noise and enable real-time decision-making.

- **Edge Continuum Concept:** The edge continuum conceptualizes the distribution of resources and software assets between centralized computing clusters and deployed nodes and sensors in the theater. This approach allows for positioning key services and analytics along the continuum, providing a significant decision advantage while alleviating bandwidth constraints.

- **Four-Layer Architecture:** The proposed architecture comprises four distinct layers:
  - **Tactical Edge:** Consists of various sensors operating in DDIL mode with limited size, weight, and power (SWaP).
  - **Operational Edge:** Bridges the Tactical and Command Edge layers, providing the first layer of sensor fusion.
  - **Command Edge:** Collects processed data from multiple Operational Edge devices, processing high-velocity and varied data from different sensors.

     o **Strategic/Enterprise Edge:** Responsible for receiving and analyzing data processed by the Command Edge layer, providing infrastructure for data storage, analysis, and decision-making.

Analysis

The proposed four-layer edge computing architecture offers several advantages for military operations:

- **Enhanced Real-Time Decision Making:** By processing data closer to the source, the architecture enables faster analysis and decision-making, crucial in time-sensitive military scenarios.

- **Improved Efficiency in DDIL Environments:** The distributed nature of the architecture allows for continued operations in denied, disrupted, intermittent, and limited-bandwidth network environments.

- **Scalability and Flexibility:** The layered approach allows for scalability across different operational levels and domains, from tactical to strategic.

- **Reduced Data Bottlenecks:** By filtering and processing data at lower levels, the architecture reduces the strain on communication networks and centralized computing resources.

- **Support for JADC2 Strategy:** The architecture aligns with the DOD's vision for integrated

command-and-control capabilities across all
domains, theaters, and threats.

Recommendations

- **Implement Pilot Programs:** Conduct small-scale
  pilot programs to test the effectiveness of the four-
  layer architecture in various operational scenarios.

- **Invest in Edge AI Technologies:** Allocate
  resources to develop and deploy AI and machine
  learning models optimized for edge computing in
  military applications.

- **Enhance Cybersecurity Measures:** Develop robust
  security protocols to protect the distributed edge
  computing infrastructure from cyber threats and
  attacks.

- **Cross-Domain Integration:** Focus on integrating
  the architecture across different military domains
  to fully realize the benefits of joint all-domain
  operations.

- **Training and Education:** Implement
  comprehensive training programs to ensure
  personnel at all levels can effectively utilize and
  maintain the new edge computing infrastructure.

Conclusion

The proposed four-layer edge computing architecture
presents a promising approach to operationalizing AI and

the edge continuum for joint military operations. By addressing data bottlenecks, enabling real-time decision-making, and supporting operations in challenging network environments, this architecture has the potential to significantly enhance the DOD's command-and-control capabilities across all domains. As the military continues to navigate increasingly complex and data-intensive operational environments, adopting such advanced computing architectures will be crucial in maintaining strategic and tactical advantages.

Further Reading

Cartwright, J. E., & Kandasamy, J. (2023). Operationalizing Artificial Intelligence and the Edge Continuum for Joint All-Domain Dominance: Unpacking a Four-Layer Architecture. Atlantic Council.

Department of Defense. (2022). Summary of the Joint All-Domain Command & Control (JADC2) Strategy. US Department of Defense.

Nix, D., & Tangredi, S. J. (2023). AI at the Edge of Chaos: Artificial Intelligence and Military Decision-Making. Naval War College Review.

Pellerin, C. (2022). DOD's Artificial Intelligence Strategy: Exploiting AI's Potential. Defense One.

Sayler, K. M. (2023). Artificial Intelligence and National Security. Congressional Research Service.

FORTY

Adapting the European Union AI Act to deal with generative artificial intelligence

Bruegal, J. Scott Marcus, 19th July 2023

This report analyzes the necessary adaptations to the European Union's AI Act to address the emergence of generative artificial intelligence, particularly foundation models. The current draft, proposed in April 2021, needs to adequately account for these powerful AI systems' unique characteristics and potential risks. We examine the challenges posed by foundation models, propose modifications to the AI Act, and recommend a balanced approach that mitigates risks while fostering innovation in the EU's AI sector.

Key Takeaways:

- The AI Act's risk-based approach is ill-suited for foundation models, which can be adapted for various uses with different risk profiles.

- A distinction between systemically important and non-systemically important foundation models could help balance regulation and innovation.

- Clearer guidelines on the use of copyrighted content for AI training are needed.

- Third-party oversight and international standards are crucial for effective regulation of foundation models.

- Enhanced safety and security measures are necessary for providers of systemically important foundation models.

The European Union's proposed AI Act, aimed at establishing harmonized rules for artificial intelligence, was drafted before the emergence of powerful generative AI tools like ChatGPT. As a result, the current draft needs to be equipped to address the unique challenges and opportunities presented by foundation models that underlie generative AI. This report examines the necessary adaptations to the AI Act to effectively regulate these advanced AI systems while supporting innovation in the EU's AI sector.

Key Findings

- **Limitations of the Current AI Act:** The AI Act's risk-based approach, which categorizes AI applications based on intended use, is not well-suited for foundation models. These models can be easily customized for various applications, each with its own risk characteristics, making it difficult to assign a single risk category.

- **Proposed Modifications by the European Parliament:** The European Parliament has

suggested new obligations for providers of
foundation models, including risk identification,
testing, and documentation. While these are steps
in the right direction, they lack detail and clarity,
and could potentially be overly burdensome for
smaller providers.

- **Need for a Differentiated Approach:** To avoid
  impeding innovation and consolidating market
  dominance of leading firms, a distinction should be
  made between systemically important and non-
  systemically important foundation models. This
  approach would allow for more stringent
  regulation of high-impact models while reducing
  burdens on smaller providers.

- **Copyright and Training Data:** The AI Act should
  clarify the permitted uses of copyrighted content
  for training foundation models and establish
  conditions for royalty payments. This would
  address ongoing uncertainties despite existing
  copyright exceptions for text and data mining.

- **Third-Party Oversight:** Given the potential
  systemic risks of advanced foundation models,
  consideration should be given to pre-market
  auditing and post-deployment evaluations by
  external experts. However, due to the scarcity of
  qualified experts, leveraging the work of
  researchers and civil society could be a viable
  alternative.

264 • AI DIGEST VOL 1

Analysis

The proposed modifications to the AI Act represent a necessary evolution in EU AI regulation. By distinguishing between systemically important and non-systemically important foundation models, the EU can create a more nuanced regulatory framework that addresses the risks posed by powerful AI systems while still fostering innovation and competition.

The clarification of copyright issues for AI training data is crucial for both AI developers and content creators. This will help establish a fair and transparent ecosystem for AI development while protecting intellectual property rights.

The implementation of third-party oversight and internationally agreed standards will be essential for ensuring the safety and reliability of foundation models. These measures can help build public trust in AI systems and facilitate international cooperation in AI governance.

Recommendations

- **Implement a Tiered Regulatory Approach:** Adopt a differentiated regulatory framework for foundation models based on their systemic importance. This will allow for more targeted and proportionate regulation.

- **Clarify Copyright Guidelines:** Amend the EU Copyright Directive to provide clear guidelines on the use of copyrighted material for AI training, including conditions for royalty payments.

- **Establish International Standards:** Work with international partners to develop agreed-upon frameworks and technical standards for identifying and assessing systemically important foundation models.

- **Enhance Safety and Security Requirements:** Mandate robust safety and security measures for providers of systemically important foundation models, including internal safeguards and external security protocols.

- **Promote Transparency and Accountability:** Implement a mandatory incident reporting procedure for foundation model providers to enhance transparency and facilitate ongoing assessment of AI risks.

Conclusion

The EU's AI Act requires significant adaptation to effectively address the challenges and opportunities presented by generative AI and foundation models. By implementing a more nuanced regulatory approach, clarifying copyright issues, establishing international standards, and enhancing safety and security requirements, the EU can create a regulatory framework that protects against potential harms while fostering innovation in the AI sector.

As a major deployer of generative AI, the EU has the potential to shape the development of this technology in alignment with its values. However, care must be taken to avoid overly burdensome regulations that could handicap EU-based AI developers. By striking the right balance, the EU can position itself as a leader in responsible AI development and deployment.

Further Reading

Marcus, J. S. (2023). Adapting the European Union AI Act to deal with generative artificial intelligence. Bruegel.

Bommasani, R., et al. (2021). On the Opportunities and Risks of Foundation Models. arXiv.

European Commission. (2021). Proposal for a Regulation laying down harmonized rules on artificial intelligence (Artificial Intelligence Act).

OECD. (2023). AI language models: Technological, socio-economic and policy considerations. OECD Digital Economy Papers.

Carugati, C. (2023). Competition in generative artificial intelligence foundation models. Bruegel Working Paper.

FORTY ONE

The environmental dark side of digitalization: an urban perspective

Barcelona Centre for International Affairs, Ricardo Martinex, July 2023

This report analyzes the environmental impact of digitalization from an urban perspective, highlighting the often-overlooked "dark side" of the digital transition. While digital technologies are often seen as key allies in the fight against climate change, they also contribute significantly to carbon emissions and other environmental damages. As primary hubs of consumption in an increasingly urbanized world, cities play a crucial role in addressing the environmental consequences of digitalization. This report examines the challenges and opportunities for city governments in managing the growing digital carbon footprint and broader environmental impacts of the digital world.

Key Takeaways:

- The digital world produced almost 4% of global carbon emissions in 2019, surpassing civil air traffic.

- Exponential technologies like AI and blockchain, while offering sustainability benefits, also drive rising energy demand and emissions.

- Environmental impacts of digitalization extend beyond carbon to water consumption, mineral extraction, and e-waste generation.

- Cities, as primary consumption hubs, must play a pivotal role in addressing digitalization's environmental impacts.

- City governments face challenges in monitoring and regulating the decentralized production of digital services.

- Opportunities exist for cities to promote circularity in data center heat reuse and e-waste "urban mining."

As the world grapples with the urgent need for ecological transition to mitigate climate change, the role of digitalization in this process is gaining increasing attention. While digital innovation is often viewed as facilitating decarbonization efforts, the environmental "dark side" of digitalization is frequently overlooked. This report explores the environmental impact of digitalization from an urban perspective, highlighting the crucial role that city governments must play in addressing the growing carbon footprint and broader environmental consequences of the digital world.

Key Findings

- **The Digital Carbon Footprint:** The digital carbon footprint is increasing by 8% annually, with the internet accounting for 7% of global electricity use. In 2019, the digital world produced almost 4% of global carbon emissions, surpassing total emissions from civil air traffic worldwide.

- **Exponential Technologies and Energy Demand:** While offering potential sustainability benefits, exponential technologies such as AI, blockchain, and the Internet of Things contribute to rising global energy demand and carbon emissions. For example, training a single AI model can generate as much carbon as five average American cars throughout their lifetime emissions.

- **Beyond Carbon: Water, Minerals, and Waste:** The environmental impact of digitalization extends beyond carbon emissions to encompass water consumption by data centers, extraction of raw minerals for digital devices, and generation of e-waste. In 2019, 53.6 million tonnes of e-waste were generated globally, with projections showing this figure nearly doubling between 2014 and 2030.

- **Cities as Digital Consumption Hubs:** As primary hubs of consumption in an increasingly urbanized world, cities generate ever-growing demand for energy-intensive digital services and infrastructure. Cities account for 67-72% of global GHG emissions and 75% of world energy consumption while producing more than 80% of global GDP.

- **Challenges in Monitoring and Regulation:** Decarbonizing cities' growing digital infrastructure is hampered by the lack of accurate data at the local level. Due to the geographically decentralized production of digital services and the opacity of supply chains, city governments struggle to assess and reduce the carbon footprint of digital services consumed within their jurisdictions.

Analysis

The environmental impact of digitalization presents a complex challenge for urban policymakers. While digital technologies offer potential solutions for sustainability, they also contribute significantly to carbon emissions and other environmental damages. Cities, as primary hubs of digital consumption, are at the forefront of this challenge.

The decentralized nature of digital services production and the opacity of supply chains make it difficult for city governments to accurately assess and regulate the environmental impact of digitalization within their jurisdictions. This calls for multi-level and multi-actor alliances, with active collaboration from private sector actors, to effectively monitor and address the digital carbon footprint in and between cities.

Despite these challenges, cities have unique opportunities to promote circularity in the digital economy. The increasing presence of data centers in urban areas offers the potential to reuse the heat generated by these facilities, contributing to cities' green energy transitions. Additionally, the concentration of e-waste in urban areas presents opportunities for "urban mining" of valuable materials, promoting a circular economy approach to electronic devices.

Recommendations

- **Develop Multi-Stakeholder Alliances:** Foster partnerships between city governments, private sector actors, and other stakeholders to improve transparency and data sharing on the environmental impacts of digital services.

- **Implement Data Center Heat Recovery:** Encourage and facilitate the reuse of heat generated by urban data centers for district heating or other purposes, following examples like the Stockholm Data Parks initiative.

- **Promote Urban Mining of E-Waste:** Develop policies and infrastructure to support the safe collection, recycling, and resource extraction from e-waste, creating new job opportunities in the circular economy.

- **Enhance Reporting Mechanisms:** Establish robust reporting frameworks for digital service providers to disclose their environmental impacts, including energy consumption and carbon emissions.

- **Invest in Research and Innovation:** Support research into more energy-efficient digital technologies and circular economy solutions for the tech sector.

Conclusion

As the environmental impacts of an increasingly digital urban world grow, city governments must take a proactive role in addressing this challenge. By leveraging their unique position as hubs of consumption and leaders in climate action, cities can play a vital role in shaping a more sustainable digital future. However, effective action will require collaboration across multiple levels of government, engagement with the private sector, and innovative approaches to promote circularity in the digital economy.

Further Reading

Martinez, R. (2023). The environmental dark side of digitalization: an urban perspective. Barcelona Centre for International Affairs.

Forti, V., et al. (2020). The Global E-waste Monitor 2020: Quantities, flows and the circular economy potential. United Nations University.

Schwarzer, S. & Peduzzi, P. (2021). The growing footprint of digitalization. UNEP Foresight Brief.

Itten, R., et al. (2020). Digital transformation—life cycle assessment of digital services, multifunctional devices and cloud computing. The International Journal of Life Cycle Assessment.

Castán Broto, V. (2021). The European Green Deal and the challenge of systemic change in urban areas. In H. Abdullah (Ed.), Towards a European Green Deal with Cities. CIDOB.

Index

www.ingramcontent.com/pod-product-compliance
Lightning Source LLC
Chambersburg PA
CBHW071237050326
40690CB00011B/2155